**New Directions for
Community Colleges**

Arthur M. Cohen
EDITOR-IN-CHIEF

Florence B. Brawer
Richard L. Wagoner
ASSOCIATE EDITORS

Carrie B. Kisker
Edward Francis Ryan
MANAGING EDITORS

Rural Community Colleges:
Teaching, Learning, and Leading in the Heartland

Pamela L. Eddy
John P. Murray
EDITORS

Number 137 • Spring 2007
Jossey-Bass
San Francisco

RURAL COMMUNITY COLLEGES: TEACHING, LEARNING, AND LEADING IN THE HEARTLAND
Pamela L. Eddy, John P. Murray (eds.)
New Directions for Community Colleges, no. 137

Arthur M. Cohen, Editor-in-Chief
Florence B. Brawer, Richard L. Wagoner, Associate Editors

NEW DIRECTIONS FOR COMMUNITY COLLEGES (ISSN 0194-3081, electronic ISSN 1536-0733) is part of The Jossey-Bass Higher and Adult Education Series and is published quarterly by Wiley Subscription Services, Inc., A Wiley Company, at Jossey-Bass, 989 Market Street, San Francisco, California 94103-1741. Periodicals Postage Paid at San Francisco, California, and at additional mailing offices. POSTMASTER: Send address changes to New Directions for Community Colleges, Jossey-Bass, 989 Market Street, San Francisco, California 94103-1741.

SUBSCRIPTIONS cost $80.00 for individuals and $195.00 for institutions, agencies, and libraries in the United States. Prices subject to change. See order form at the back of book.

EDITORIAL CORRESPONDENCE should be sent to the Editor-in-Chief, Arthur M. Cohen, at the Graduate School of Education and Information Studies, University of California, Box 951521, Los Angeles, California 90095-1521. All manuscripts receive anonymous reviews by external referees.

New Directions for Community Colleges is indexed in Current Index to Journals in Education (ERIC).

Microfilm copies of issues and articles are available in 16mm and 35mm, as well as microfiche in 105mm, through University Microfilms Inc., 300 North Zeeb Road, Ann Arbor, Michigan 48106-1346.

CONTENTS

THE WILEY BICENTENNIAL–KNOWLEDGE FOR GENERATIONS

*E*ach generation has its unique needs and aspirations. When Charles Wiley first opened his small printing shop in lower Manhattan in 1807, it was a generation of boundless potential searching for an identity. And we were there, helping to define a new American literary tradition. Over half a century later, in the midst of the Second Industrial Revolution, it was a generation focused on building the future. Once again, we were there, supplying the critical scientific, technical, and engineering knowledge that helped frame the world. Throughout the 20th Century, and into the new millennium, nations began to reach out beyond their own borders and a new international community was born. Wiley was there, expanding its operations around the world to enable a global exchange of ideas, opinions, and know-how.

For 200 years, Wiley has been an integral part of each generation's journey, enabling the flow of information and understanding necessary to meet their needs and fulfill their aspirations. Today, bold new technologies are changing the way we live and learn. Wiley will be there, providing you the must-have knowledge you need to imagine new worlds, new possibilities, and new opportunities.

Generations come and go, but you can always count on Wiley to provide you the knowledge you need, when and where you need it!

WILLIAM J. PESCE
PRESIDENT AND CHIEF EXECUTIVE OFFICER

PETER BOOTH WILEY
CHAIRMAN OF THE BOARD

EDITORS' NOTES

The recent reconfiguration of the Carnegie classification system for insti-tutions of higher education (Carnegie Foundation for the Advancement of Teaching, 2006) created distinctions between community colleges based on location and size, allowing scholars and practitioners to empirically exam-ine for the first time what many have known for years: that community col-leges vary tremendously by geographic location and size. One new category in the Carnegie system is rural community colleges. Rural community col-leges make up 60 percent of all two-year institutions and educate one-third of all community college students each year. Rural community colleges are defined as public two-year institutions with a physical address outside the hundred largest standard or consolidated metropolitan statistical areas. Small rural community colleges are those with enrollments under twenty-five hundred students, community colleges with enrollments between twenty-five hundred and five thousand are midsized, and those with enroll-ments greater than seventy-five hundred are considered large (Katsinas, 2003). Although, clearly, rural institutions make up a sizable percentage of all two-year colleges, often community college headlines focus on urban or large colleges rather than small and more remote ones. Many of the issues community colleges face—such as greater need for remediation, changing student demographics, use of technology in the classroom, and pending retirements of faculty and leaders—are faced by both urban and rural col-leges, but in the rural context these issues play out differently. Understand-ing better how issues and challenges are different in rural colleges certainly benefits those who work and study in rural institutions, but it benefits those in urban and suburban colleges as well, because they may learn from their rural counterparts' successful tactics and approaches to the complex issues all colleges face.

As community colleges gain greater national and political attention, it is important not to overlook rural colleges and to think about how these institutions can meet the demands placed on them. In planning for the future, should rural community colleges try to concentrate on certain mis-sions—such as transfer education or distance learning—or should they con-tinue trying to be all things to all people? In this area, urban and suburban community colleges face similar institutional dilemmas and choices and can learn from the experiences of rural colleges.

This volume explores what it means to lead, teach in, partner with, or attend rural community colleges. Challenges for community colleges include attracting and retaining faculty and selecting leaders who understand

NEW DIRECTIONS FOR COMMUNITY COLLEGES, no. 137, Spring 2007 © 2007 Wiley Periodicals, Inc.
Published online in Wiley InterScience (www.interscience.wiley.com) • DOI: 10.1002/cc.264

1

the unique issues that two-year colleges face—including resource constraints, stagnant economies, and isolated service areas. Recruiting and retaining rural community college faculty and leaders are also a challenge because of the lack of amenities in these more remote regions of the country. Faculty are often the sole persons responsible for their discipline, which results in a lack of support from peers and singular responsibility for teaching the discipline. This often means multiple preparations every academic term. In addition, students are affected by the lack of faculty diversity because—with the exception of some adjunct faculty—the only voice they hear on a particular topic is that of a single faculty member. Administrators and faculty must also live in areas with fewer cultural amenities, areas that are often located at a great distance from the state capital—critical for lobbying efforts and statewide meetings. They face the challenge of leading a smaller institution with fewer resources and greater economic constraints. Yet leaders of rural colleges are still expected to meet the community college's tripartite mission of preparing students for transfer to four-year institutions, educating the workforce, and aiding in economic development (Cohen and Brawer, 2003).

This volume of *New Directions for Community Colleges* should be useful to those leading and working in rural community colleges, community agencies and universities involved in partnerships with rural community colleges, college members of the Rural Community College Alliance and the Rural Community College Initiative, and those interested in understanding the role geographic context plays on community college campuses. In addition, the volume provides institutional researchers with a better understanding of the demographics and pressing personnel issues faced by rural community colleges, and offers potential rural college leaders and faculty knowledge about how to prepare for their roles at these institutions. As well, university educators and researchers with an interest in community colleges will benefit from this important addition to the community college research base.

Chapter One, by David Hardy and Stephen Katsinas, provides a context for the issues rural community colleges face by describing how these institutions differ from their urban and suburban counterparts, as well as how small, medium, and large rural colleges differ from each other. Chapter Two describes what Charles Fluharty and Bill Scaggs term the "rural differential"—the chronic underfunding of rural community colleges in comparison to those in urban and suburban areas—and discusses the corresponding challenges this gap causes in maintaining campus operations, generating philanthropic donations, and fulfilling the rural college mission.

Chapter Three, by Michael Miller and Daniel Kissinger, explores how rural community colleges work with their surrounding communities. Rural community colleges play a different role in regional economic development than urban institutions, which have more partners available to help in renewal efforts. In rural communities, the two-year college is often the largest employer and the entity to which others turn for help in developing the economy. In recent years, many rural areas have experienced declining populations as the traditional agricultural base continues to shift to fewer, larger farms and people move to urban areas or retire to sunnier climes. As well, recent economic downturns have increased pressure on rural two-year colleges to aid in economic development, often resulting in an increasingly important role for these colleges in their local communities. Chapter Three discusses these challenges and describes how rural community colleges can contribute to their communities' sense of identity formation and engagement through continuing education programs and other noncredit activities.

The next two chapters focus on issues related to rural community college leadership. Research shows that community college presidents lead a campus for an average of five years (Corrigan, 2002) and that we are anticipating a shortage of leaders to replace the 70 percent of presidents who plan to retire within the next ten years (Shults, 2001). With a national demand for community college presidential replacements, how will rural colleges attract and compete for new leaders? Fewer cultural events, lower pay, and isolated locations all create challenges and impediments for attracting and retaining rural college leaders. Chapter Four, written by Jay Leist, describes these issues and details how rural community colleges can create accurate and informative presidential job advertisements that will enable a better fit between presidential candidates and rural colleges. Chapter Five, written by Molly Clark and Ed Davis, takes another tack, describing how rural colleges can establish partnerships with universities to create programming that will help locally develop and enhance the leadership needed in rural locales. Specifically, Chapter Five describes the MidSouth Community College Fellowship Program and best practices in leadership development.

Chapters Six and Seven then turn to issues related to rural community college faculty. In Chapter Six John Murray describes challenges specific to teaching in rural locations and discusses how rural colleges can better recruit and retain faculty members. Chapter Seven, written by Pamela Eddy, addresses the fact that faculty in rural community colleges, although few in number, are still responsible for keeping up to date on teaching pedagogies, particularly in how technology affects student learning. Therefore, access to professional development and resources to support professors as they stay current in the field are critical. Chapter Seven discusses these issues, and highlights the challenges many rural community colleges face in providing effective faculty development programs.

Chapters Eight and Nine discuss issues of critical importance to many rural community colleges: on-campus student housing and distance education. At rural community colleges, students must often commute longer distances than their urban counterparts do. Therefore, although living facilities are not always associated with community colleges, many rural institutions provide on-campus housing for students. Chapter Eight, by Pat Moeck, David Hardy, and Stephen Katsinas, provides data on student housing at rural community college campuses and discusses the implications for rural colleges and their students. Chapter Nine, by Brent Cejda, reviews the importance of distance learning for rural community colleges and discusses some of the challenges these institutions face in providing online and other forms of distance education.

Chapter Ten, written by Pamela Eddy and John Murray, synthesizes lessons learned from Chapters One through Nine and describes strategies that rural community colleges can take to address the issues and challenges presented in this volume. The chapter also provides a list of sources to which practitioners and scholars can turn for more information on teaching, learning, and leading in the heartland. Taken together, the chapters in this volume provide community college leaders, faculty, staff, and scholars with a better understanding of the unique challenges and issues that rural community colleges face. Each chapter includes campus-based examples, offers best practices, or covers implications for practice and policy in a rural environment. Urban and suburban college leaders can transfer the information and best practices presented here to their institutions by applying them to an urban or suburban context.

Pamela L. Eddy
John P. Murray
Editors

References

Carnegie Foundation for the Advancement of Teaching. *The Carnegie Classification of Institutions of Higher Education.* New York: Carnegie Foundation for the Advancement of Teaching, 2006. http://www.carnegiefoundation.org/classifications. Accessed Nov. 29, 2006.

Cohen, A. M., and Brawer, F. B. *The American Community College.* (4th ed.) San Francisco: Jossey-Bass, 2003.

Corrigan, M. *The American College President, 2002 Edition.* Washington, D.C.: American Council on Education, Center for Policy Analysis, 2002.

Katsinas, S. G. "Two-Year College Classifications Based on Institutional Control, Geography, Governance, and Size." In A. McCormick and R. Cox (eds.), *Classification Systems for Two-Year Colleges.* New Directions for Community Colleges, no. 122. San Francisco: Jossey-Bass, 2003.

Shults, C. *The Critical Impact of Impending Retirements on Community College Leadership.* Leadership Series Research Brief No. 1. Washington, D.C.: American Association of Community Colleges, 2001.

PAMELA L. EDDY *is associate professor of higher education and doctoral program coordinator in education leadership at Central Michigan University.*

JOHN P. MURRAY *is professor of higher education at Texas Tech University and program director for the higher education administration program.*

1

This chapter describes rural community colleges, compares them to their urban and suburban counterparts, and highlights the unique challenges they face in the twenty-first century.

Classifying Community Colleges: How Rural Community Colleges Fit

David E. Hardy, Stephen G. Katsinas

In 1995, the *New Directions for Community Colleges* series published a volume that described the status and role of the rural community college in American higher education. Titled *Portrait of the Rural Community College* (Killacky and Valadez, 1995), the chapters—although useful in illuminating issues important to practitioners at rural community colleges—provided no empirical data of a comparative nature to show how many rural community colleges exist in the United States, how many students they serve, the programs they offer, the services they provide, and their average budget size. This chapter directly addresses this deficiency by using empirical data that describe how rural community colleges differ from their suburban and urban counterparts. It also provides a context for the issues rural community college practitioners face, including those presented in the following chapters.

In the early 1990s, when Stephen Katsinas and Vincent Lacey (1996) began their work on the classification of two-year colleges, it was not easy for researchers to manipulate large computer databases created by the federal government, including the U.S. Department of Education's Integrated Postsecondary Education Data System (IPEDS). The resultant inability to disaggregate community colleges by institutional type served to paper over differences among two-year colleges in terms of governance (single versus multicampus systems) and geographic area (rural, suburban, or urban). Today, however, it *is* possible to disaggregate data by community college type using IPEDS and other national databases. Using the Carnegie Foundation

for the Advancement of Teaching's (2006a, 2006b) new Basic Classifications, which are based on Hardy's 2005 update to the Katsinas and Lacey classification system for two-year colleges, this chapter presents data on different types of community colleges, their student populations, the availability of various curricular offerings and student support services, levels and types of financial support and expenditures, and variations in student aid in order to highlight the differences between rural community colleges and other two-year institutions. The chapter concludes with some thoughts about how the new classification scheme will affect policy and practice.

The New 2005 Carnegie Classifications

For the first time, the Carnegie Foundation for the Advancement of Teaching's 2005 Basic Classifications provide multiple classifications for colleges offering the associate degree. Prior classification schemas aggregated all two-year colleges into a single category. The 2005 Basic Classifications divide associate degree–granting colleges into three major categories: publicly controlled, privately controlled, and special-use institutions. Under the privately controlled category are private, nonprofit junior colleges and proprietary institutions, and under the special-use category are specialized two-year colleges, such as hospital-based radiography and nursing programs, some of which are publicly controlled. The public category includes the subcategories of rural, suburban, and urban-serving colleges, as well as two-year colleges governed by four-year institutions. In the urban and suburban categories, the institutions are subdivided into single and multicampus districts; in the rural category, the institutions are divided by size into small, medium, and large rural colleges (see Table 1.1).

Carnegie's 2005 Basic Classifications use the suffix *serving* to its rural, suburban, and urban categories, reflecting the reality that nearly all public community colleges are place-based institutions, with geographic service delivery areas defined by state statute, regulation, or custom. Institutions are placed according to the physical address they supply the U.S. Department of Education and the Census Bureau. The word *serving* thus reflects that these institutions primarily serve students from urban, suburban, and rural areas, depending on the physical location of that campus (Carnegie Foundation for the Advancement of Teaching, 2006a, 2006b), but it is recognized that these institutions also may serve some populations in other geographic designations. For the purpose of brevity, instead of using the Carnegie nomenclature of *rural-serving* community colleges, we will use the term *rural community colleges* in this chapter.

The 2005 Basic Classifications address Townsend's (2002) concern that two-year colleges need to be viewed through frames appropriate to two-year colleges, and not by applying four-year college frames to two-year institutions. This is achieved by using annual unduplicated head count, rather than full-time equivalent (FTE) students, to classify colleges. Practitioners

Table 1.1. Two-Year Colleges by Campus and District, Mean Enrollment by Campus and District, 2000–01

College Type	Number of Districts	Number of Campuses	Mean Enrollment per District	Mean Enrollment per Campus
I. Publicly controlled two-year colleges	896	1,666	10,813	5,816
Rural colleges/districts	553	922	5,812	3,486
Small (<2,500 annual unduplicated head count)	140	206	1,699	1,155
Medium (2,500 to 7,500 annual unduplicated enrollment)	303	499	4,642	2,819
Large (>7,500 annual unduplicated enrollment)	110	217	14,269	7,233
Suburban colleges/districts	195	328	15,528	9,232
Single campus districts	122	122	12,002	12,002
Multicampus districts	73	206	21,421	7,591
Urban colleges/districts	112	302	28,401	10,533
Single campus districts	44	44	12,947	12,947
Multicampus districts	68	258	38,402	10,122
Total publicly controlled two-year community and technical colleges	860	1,552	10,957	6,072
Two-year colleges governed by four-year universities	36	114	7,380	2,331
II. Privately controlled two-year colleges	825	825	705	705
III. Special-use two-year colleges	43	138	2,183	680
All two-year colleges	1,764	2,629	6,137	4,050

planning parking lots, computers, classrooms, and libraries think in terms of human beings, and not FTEs, reflecting the substantially different usage patterns for community college facilities compared to their four-year counterparts. Annual total unduplicated head count is a much more accurate and appropriate measure of the reach of community colleges.

Rural Community Colleges and Their Students

Among public community colleges, student enrollments are evenly distributed across the rural, suburban, and urban subcategories. A total of 3,213,977

NEW DIRECTIONS FOR COMMUNITY COLLEGES • DOI: 10.1002/cc

students attended rural community colleges in 2000–01, compared to 3,027,986 at suburban and 3,181,009 at urban community colleges. In other words, 34 percent of the nation's community college students attend rural institutions, 32 percent attend suburban colleges, and 34 percent attend urban community colleges. The majority of rural community college campuses (72 percent) are located in the north central and southern accrediting regions (Hardy, 2005).

A key implication for policy and practice of this large number of rural community colleges is that greater variability of institutional types exists among rural colleges compared to their urban and suburban counterparts. In the suburban and urban categories, single-campus districts are roughly the same size (mean enrollment is 12,002 for suburban districts, and 12,947 for urban districts), although multicampus districts range in size from 21,421 students in suburban colleges to 38,402 in urban institutions. All urban and suburban campuses are quite large compared to rural institutions; the smallest mean campus enrollment in the suburban and urban college categories (7,591 at campuses in suburban multicampus districts) is larger than the mean enrollment at large rural community colleges (7,233 students).

Although two-thirds of all U.S. community college students are enrolled in urban and suburban colleges, the 34 percent of students who attend the 922 identifiable rural community college campuses represent 59 percent of all community college campuses in the country. The enrollment spread is substantial: the 206 small rural campuses average an annual unduplicated head count enrollment of just 1,155 students, whereas the annual unduplicated head count is 2,819 at medium rural and 7,233 at large rural colleges. In other words, despite the large number of rural community colleges, urban and suburban multicampus districts serve over 40 percent of all U.S. community college students. In the rural category, nearly half (49 percent) are enrolled in the 110 large rural community college districts, 44 percent are enrolled in the 303 medium rural community college districts, and 7 percent are enrolled in the 140 small rural community college districts.

In 1978, Arthur M. Cohen argued that, lacking an empirical method by which to disaggregate community colleges, size was the most accurate single determining factor. For example, large rural and suburban community colleges are quite similar in terms of organizational complexity and range of curricular offerings. In contrast, whereas only 7 percent of rural community college students attend small institutions (with enrollments below 2,500), these 140 colleges are quite different from their suburban and urban counterparts. Small rural districts enroll an average of 1,699 students; the average campus enrollment is 1,155 (Hardy, 2005). At these small rural institutions, staff and faculty are likely to perform many different administrative functions, and the curriculum is necessarily narrower than that offered at a suburban campus that is ten times its size. It is very clear that, in terms of size and complexity of the programs offered, there is substantially greater variation in the rural community college category than in the urban or suburban categories. These differences have important implications for state policymakers who wish to use rural community colleges to deliver regional workforce training. The economies of scale that exist for the delivery of workforce training at urban and suburban community colleges (and even large rural community colleges) may not exist at the 140 small rural community colleges, and are also unlikely at many of the 303 medium rural community colleges.

By race and ethnicity of students enrolled, rural community colleges differ greatly from urban and suburban community colleges, and there are also differences within the rural category itself (see Table 1.2). For example, white students account for 45 percent of all urban, 54 percent of all suburban, and 74 percent of all rural community college enrollments. This means that most of the nation's 112 urban community college districts have majority-minority enrollments, and many suburban community colleges likely do as well. In contrast, few rural community colleges are majority-minority.

African American students make up the largest minority group in rural community colleges, yet their representation varies across college type. Nationally, African American students account for 14 percent of all U.S. community college students (U.S. Department of Education, 2006). However, in the three rural community college subcategories, African American students account for 20 percent of small, 10 percent of medium, and 6 percent of large rural community colleges students. Rural community colleges in the Southeast have substantially larger proportions of African American students than rural colleges in the Midwest and other regions.

Similarly, although 15 percent of all community college students in America are Hispanic, only 7 percent of students attending rural colleges

Table 1.2. Percentage of Student Enrollment at Publicly Controlled Two-Year Community and Technical Colleges by Race and Ethnicity, 2000–01

College Type (Percent of Students)	African American	American Indian/ Alaskan Native	Asian/ Pacific Islander	Hispanic	White	Nonresident Alien	Race Unknown
Rural	9	1	2	7	74	1	4
Small	20	1	1	2	72	0	3
Medium	10	1	1	5	77	0	4
Large	6	2	3	10	72	1	5
Suburban	9	1	11	15	54	2	8
Urban	16	1	9	21	45	2	6

NEW DIRECTIONS FOR COMMUNITY COLLEGES • DOI: 10.1002/cc

are from a Hispanic or Latino background. On average, Hispanic students represent a greater percentage of total enrollment at large rural community colleges (10 percent) than at small and medium rural colleges (2 and 5 percent, respectively). Likewise, Asian students make up 9 and 11 percent of enrollments at urban and suburban community colleges, respectively, but only 2 percent at rural community colleges.

As Table 1.3 illustrates, substantially different enrollment patterns exist at rural community colleges than at their urban and suburban counterparts, and there is also variability in the rural category. Rural community colleges serve significantly larger percentages of full-time students (41 percent) than suburban (32 percent) or urban (31 percent) community colleges. In the three rural subcategories, the percentages of full- and part-time students are strikingly different. At the 110 large rural community college districts, the percentages of full-time students resemble those at suburban and urban community colleges; 36 percent of students are enrolled full-time and 64 percent are enrolled part-time. In contrast, at the 303 medium rural community college districts, 45 percent of students are enrolled full-time and 55 percent are enrolled part-time. At the 140 small rural community college districts, 50 percent are enrolled full-time and 50 percent are enrolled part-time. The higher percentages of full-time students at medium and small rural community college districts may indicate that these institutions serve larger numbers of students in nursing, allied

Table 1.3. Percentage Unduplicated Credit Enrollment by Gender and Enrollment Status at Publicly Controlled Two-Year Community and Technical Colleges, 2000–01

College Type (Percent Enrollment)	Full-Time Enrollment (Male/Female)	Part-Time Enrollment (Male/Female)
Rural	41	59
	(45/55)	(41/59)
Small	50	50
	(44/56)	(39/61)
Medium	45	55%
	(44/56)	(40/60)
Large	36	64
	(46/54)	(42/58)
Suburban	32	68
	(46/54)	(43/57)
Urban	31	69
	(44/56)	(43/57)

health, and technical education programs (such as automotive technology) that generally require full-time enrollment, or that they serve more students in traditional transfer curricula leading to the associate degree. Also, the availability of residential halls at many medium and small rural community colleges may result in higher full-time enrollments (according to Moeck, 2005, 90 percent of the 232 community colleges offering on-campus housing are rural institutions).

When we examine the data by gender and enrollment status, similarities and differences between types of community colleges and in the three rural categories can be observed (see again Table 1.3). In general, rural community colleges enroll greater percentages of full-time students than their urban and suburban counterparts (41, 31, and 32 percent, respectively). Further, in the rural category, the smaller the college the higher the percentage of full-time students. Despite this difference, the male-female balance across all types of colleges is relatively stable. For example, 56 and 54 percent of full-time students served at urban and suburban community colleges, respectively, are female. Similarly, 55 percent of full-time students at rural community colleges are female. Females make up 59, 57, and 57 percent, respectively, of part-time students at rural, suburban, and urban community colleges.

Not surprisingly, given their higher enrollment numbers at all types of community colleges, women earn 63 percent of all associate degrees; this statistic is fairly consistent across all types of community colleges (Hardy, 2005). It is clear that America's community colleges, regardless of type, are majority-female institutions and that increasing the numbers and percentages of male students will likely be a challenge for some time to come. Interestingly, males represent slightly smaller percentages of part-time enrollments at small rural community colleges than at larger rural institutions or urban and suburban colleges. As noted in the preceding pages, this may be because the vocational programs offered at these small rural colleges generally require full-time enrollment.

It is also important to note the difference in mean enrollment among urban, suburban, and rural community colleges, as well as differences in the rural subcategory. The mean enrollment in fall 2000 at urban and suburban community colleges was 6,288 and 5,443, respectively. This compares to a mean enrollment of 2,100 across all types of rural community colleges. In the three rural subcategories, large rural colleges had a mean enrollment of 4,126 in 2000, compared with 1,757 at medium and 761 at small rural community colleges. These enrollment data suggest that small and medium rural colleges may be hard-pressed to offer the broad range of economic development and workforce training programs and services that their large rural, suburban, and urban counterparts are able to deliver to students who usually enroll in these programs on a part-time basis. In addition, the lower mean enrollments suggest that small and medium rural community colleges are likely challenged to simply deliver a comprehensive curriculum. Indeed, Reid (2006) found that of the eighteen public community and six tribal community colleges invited to participate in the Ford Foundation's Rural Community College Initiative (1994 to 2003), only seventeen had nursing and allied health programs. These data call into question the ability of small rural community colleges to offer a comprehensive, broad-based curriculum to their students, a reality that is taken for granted at many of the nation's public community colleges in urban and suburban areas. Also, the much higher presence of intercollegiate athletics at large rural community colleges—81 percent have athletics, compared with 70 and 62 percent, respectively, at suburban and urban community colleges—might account for the greater percentage of full-time enrollments at rural colleges (Castañeda, 2004).

Rural Curricular Offerings and Student Support Services

Although medium and large rural community colleges offer similar educational and student services programs as colleges located in urban and suburban areas, only 80 percent of small rural colleges offer an academic program of study (see Table 1.4). However, virtually all rural colleges offer occupational programs, and all provide remedial and tutoring services for their students (as do all urban and suburban community colleges). As well, most rural colleges (87 percent) offer Adult Basic Education (ABE) or General Educational Development (GED) preparation, although this percentage is slightly less than that at urban colleges (92 percent). All rural community colleges offer academic and career counseling services to their students, and most provide both employment services for students and placement services for program completers. In addition, 92 percent of all large rural community colleges offer recreational and avocational programs for their communities, which is a significantly higher percentage than at any other type of community college; only 76 and 73 percent, respectively, of suburban and urban colleges offer these programs.

However, not all rural colleges are alike in offering recreational and avocational programs. Small rural colleges are much less likely than their larger counterparts to offer these activities. This suggests that large rural institutions may be serving as fine arts and recreational *hubs* for their regions; small rural community colleges may not have the resources necessary to benefit from the economy of scale necessary to offer this kind of curricular and community programming. Unfortunately, however, there also appears to be scant financial support for such activities. For example, in a recent analysis of National Endowment for the Arts (NEA) grant making, Terry, Hardy, and Katsinas (2006) found that the NEA awarded just $3,200 to all of Alabama's twenty-seven community colleges between 2000 and 2003. Public policy supporting rural community colleges in providing recreational and avocational programming for this role clearly appears to be limited.

Table 1.4. Percentage of Publicly Controlled Two-Year Community and Technical Colleges Offering Various Educational and Student Services Programs, 2000–01

Programs Offered (Percent Offering)	Rural	Small Rural	Medium Rural	Large Rural	Suburban	Urban	Total
Academic programs	93	80	95	99	96	98	94
Occupational programs	98	96	98	100	98	98	98
Remedial/tutoring services	100	100	100	100	100	100	100
ABE/GED	87	82	87	93	86	92	88
Academic/career counseling	100	100	100	100	100	100	100
Employment services for current students	93	86	93	99	97	94	94
Placement services for program completers	90	84	91	94	84	94	90
Recreational/avocational programs	72	50	72	92	76	73	73
Accelerated programs	22	10	20	38	30	46	28
Work-study	60	51	58	76	63	67	62
Distance learning	86	67	90	94	88	86	86
Study abroad	13	4	9	28	32	33	21
ROTC	5	1	3	13	12	22	10
Teacher preparation/ certification	4	2	3	7	9	8	6
Classes on weekends	20	7	22	29	41	45	29
On-campus child care for students	47	26	46	70	67	75	57
Middle college/high school diploma programs	11	12	8	16	11	11	11

Small rural community colleges also are less likely (10 percent) than medium and large rural institutions (20 and 38 percent, respectively) or urban and suburban community colleges (46 and 30 percent, respectively) to offer accelerated learning options. They are also less likely to offer work-study or distance learning(see again Table 1.4). As well, fewer rural colleges, especially the smaller ones, provide study abroad or teacher preparation programs for their students. Finally, rural community colleges are less likely to offer classes on the weekends than other types of two-year colleges (20 percent of all rural community colleges offer weekend courses, compared with 41 and 45 percent, respectively, of suburban and urban community colleges).

These data likely reflect the much smaller budgets of rural community colleges. According to Roessler (2006), rural community colleges had an average total budget of $23.4 million in fiscal year 2001, compared with $50.2 and $102.4 million, respectively, at suburban and urban community college districts. Furthermore, small rural community college districts had an average budget size of $9.9 million compared to $20.4 and $48 million, respectively, for medium and large rural community college districts. It necessarily follows that the 443 small and medium rural community colleges in the United States need targeted assistance from state policymakers who wish to extend access to postsecondary education to all citizens in their states and expand lifelong learning opportunities for all citizens.

Two community college service programs deserve special note here— on-campus child care and distance education. Lack of these two services and educational options have long been cited as key challenges faced by rural community college students (Katsinas, Alexander, and Opp, 2003), although distance education and child-care programs can help students overcome barriers to college access and success. It is therefore troubling to note that few opportunities for on-campus child care exist for students at medium and small rural community colleges, and that only 67 percent of small rural community colleges offer comprehensive distance education programs.

At urban and suburban community colleges, private child-care providers are often located at nearby sites convenient to the campus, which allows colleges to shift financial and legal responsibility for child care to an off-site organization. This is made easier in many suburban and urban communities by the availability of publicly subsidized mass transit. However, mass transit is often not available in rural areas, which makes off-campus child care a less feasible alternative and compounds the problems caused by lack of on-campus child care. Providing funds for on-campus child care and extending distance learning opportunities to more rural residents are other areas of opportunity for state policymakers who desire to provide access to postsecondary education to all the citizens of their states.

Discussion and Conclusion

As this chapter has shown, the nation's 553 rural community college districts and 922 rural campuses differ significantly from their suburban and urban peers. There are important similarities among all types of community colleges, particularly in relation to the traditional community college commitment to access and open door admissions. For example, all community colleges show a commitment to social mobility by offering educational programs such as ABE, GED preparation, academic and career counseling, employment placement, and remedial and tutoring services. Yet there are also significant differences. Like other types of community colleges, rural institutions enroll more female than male students, yet rural institutions enroll higher percentages of full-time students. As well, rural colleges are less likely than their more urban counterparts to offer continuing and professional education programs, recreational or avocational courses that are not designed to lead to a degree, accelerated programs, work-study, study abroad, and enrichment programs such as credit-for-life experience. They are also less likely to offer weekend courses, ROTC, and teacher preparation programs. They generally have fewer on-campus student services, such as employment services, placement services for program completers, and on-campus child care. In general, the smaller the rural college, the less likely it is to offer these types of programs.

Small rural community colleges, in particular, differ from virtually every other institutional type in a number of ways. They are far less likely than other community colleges to offer a comprehensive mix of educational programs and student services, are more likely to rely primarily on state appropriations, and are more likely to have a higher cost per student (Roessler, 2006). As Katsinas, Alexander, and Opp (2003) have proposed, it may be necessary to consider implementing policies that increase state and federal funding (in the form of vouchers or waivers) to small rural institutions, because these institutions cannot benefit from the economies of scale that help larger institutions bring in more money and reduce per-student expenditures.

Understanding the similarities and differences between rural community colleges of different sizes, as well as between rural colleges and urban and suburban institutions, can inform local, state, and national policymakers in developing public policies that can extend access to all types of institutions and improve student outcomes. The fact is that all two-year colleges do not operate on a fiscally even playing field. More effective and equitable federal and state appropriations, as well as the development of special funding programs that address the needs of rural communities, are sorely needed. Finally, policymakers should take differences in institutional type and location into account when planning for changes in student demographics, programs to improve student readiness for college, workforce and instructional needs, and faculty retirement. Rural community colleges are unique institutions. In order to best serve their students and communities, rural college leaders and policymakers need to take these differences into account and adjust programs and practices accordingly.

In the spring of 2003 and 2004, state directors of community colleges were asked: "Which of the following types of community colleges in your state will experience the greatest fiscal strain during the 2004–05 fiscal year?" That such a strong majority reported that their rural community colleges were facing the greatest strain (25 percent, compared with 2 and 9 percent, respectively, who stated that suburban and urban colleges faced the greatest strain) strongly indicates that state-level policymakers understand the importance of economies of scale in delivering quality postsecondary education programs and services to all of the citizens of their states, including rural Americans (Katsinas and Palmer, 2003; Katsinas, Palmer, and Tollefson, 2004). However, this knowledge has not always led to an alleviation of these problems.

New Directions for Community Colleges • DOI: 10.1002/cc

This, then, is the challenge: How can America's rural community colleges—often the only institutions of higher education accessible to our most remote and disadvantaged populations—best work to achieve the curricular comprehensiveness of their urban and suburban peers? Chapters Two through Ten of this volume explore specific aspects of this complex question and pose possible solutions to the myriad problems that rural community colleges face.

References

Carnegie Foundation for the Advancement of Teaching. "Basic Classification Description." New York: Carnegie Foundation for the Advancement of Teaching, 2006a. http://www.carnegiefoundation.org/classifications/sub.asp?key=791. Accessed Nov. 28, 2006.

Carnegie Foundation for the Advancement of Teaching. "Basic Classification Technical Details." New York: Carnegie Foundation for the Advancement of Teaching, 2006b. http://www.carnegiefoundation.org/classifications/index.asp?key=798. Accessed Nov. 28, 2006.

Castañeda, C. "A National Overview of Intercollegiate Athletics in Public Community Colleges." *Dissertation Abstracts International,* 2004, 65(8), 2915A. (UMI No. AAT 3144975)

Cohen, A. M. "Current Research on Small/Rural Community Colleges: Separating Fact from Fiction." Paper presented at the first annual National Conference on Small/Rural Colleges, Blacksburg, Va., Aug. 1978. (ED 165 845)

Hardy, D. E. "A Two-Year College Typology for the 21st Century: Updating and Utilizing the Katsinas-Lacey Classification System." *Dissertation Abstracts International,* 2005, 66(7), 2508A. (UMI No. AAT 3181046)

Katsinas, S. G., Alexander, K. F., and Opp, R. D. *Preserving Access with Excellence: Financing for Rural Community Colleges.* Rural Community College Initiative Policy Paper. Chapel Hill, N.C.: MDC, Inc., 2003.

Katsinas, S. G., and Lacey, V. A. "A Classification of Community Colleges on America: A Technical Report." New York: Ford Foundation Education and Culture Program, 1996.

Katsinas, S. G., and Palmer, J. C. "State Funding for Community Colleges: A View from the Field." Denton: University of North Texas, Bill J. Priest Center for Community College Education, 2003.

Katsinas, S. G., Palmer, J. C., and Tollefson, T. A. "State Funding for Community Colleges: A View from the Field." Denton: University of North Texas, Bill J. Priest Center for Community College Education, 2004.

Killacky, J., and Valadez, J. R. (eds.). *Portrait of the Rural Community College.* New Directions for Community Colleges, no. 90. San Francisco: Jossey-Bass, 1995.

Moeck, P. G. "An Analysis of On-Campus Housing at Public Rural Community Colleges in the United States." *Dissertation Abstracts International,* 2005, 66(6), 2079. (UMI No. AAT 3181058)

Reid, M. B. "Rural Community Colleges and the Nursing Shortage in Severely Distressed Counties." *Dissertation Abstracts International,* 2006, 66(11), 3952. (UMI No. AAT 3196174)

Roessler, B. C. "A Quantitative Study of Revenues and Expenditures at U.S. Community Colleges, 1980–2001." *Dissertation Abstracts International,* 2006, 67(4), 1200. (UMI No. AAT 3214494)

Terry, S. L., Hardy, D. E., and Katsinas, S. G. "Cultural Enrichment Activities in Community Colleges: An Analysis of Government Funding and Support." Paper presented at the Council for the Study of the Community Colleges' annual conference, Long Beach, Calif., Apr. 2006.

Townsend, B. K. "Invited Panel Report on the Community College: Challenges and Pathways." Paper presented at the annual conference of the American Educational Research Association, Seattle, Apr. 2002. http://www.cscconline.org/aerapaper.pdf. Accessed Nov. 28, 2006.

U.S. Department of Education, National Center for Education Statistics. "Programs and Plans of the National Center for Education Statistics, 2005 Edition." *Education Statistics Quarterly*, 2006, 7(1, 2), n.p. http://nces.ed.gov/programs/quarterly/vol_7/1_2/2_1. asp. Accessed Nov. 28, 2006.

DAVID E. HARDY *is assistant professor of higher education and director of research for the Education Policy Center at the University of Alabama.*

STEPHEN G. KATSINAS *is director of the Education Policy Center and professor of higher education at the University of Alabama.*

NEW DIRECTIONS FOR COMMUNITY COLLEGES • DOI: 10.1002/cc

2

Rural communities have fewer financial resources, making the community colleges located in these regions central to economic development. This chapter reviews the importance of recognizing the rural differential via policy changes and offers strategies to close the resource gap between rural and nonrural community colleges.

The Rural Differential: Bridging the Resource Gap

Charles Fluharty, Bill Scaggs

Rural community colleges and their communities share a common destiny. Across our nation, these institutions provide access to educational opportunities and serve as catalysts for community and economic development. The fact that rural colleges represent 60 percent of all community colleges (Carnegie Foundation for the Advancement of Teaching, 2006) highlights the central role these institutions play across the country. However, meaningful public policies and adequate resources to achieve the simultaneous outcomes of building rural community development capacity and educating rural residents are woefully lacking. In fact, there is a substantial differential between rural community colleges and their suburban and urban counterparts. For several decades, rural institutions have received only a small percentage of the available federal community development support. Similarly, there is chronic underfunding of community colleges serving disadvantaged communities, especially those in rural areas, which results in increasingly fragile institutions serving increasingly fragile communities.

Across America, there are at least 922 rural community college campuses (Hardy and Katsinas, 2006). Incomes tend to be lower, and poverty rates higher, in these rural areas than in more urban areas. For example, the median family income in nonmetropolitan areas is only 76.8 percent of the median metropolitan family income (Miller and Rowley, 2002). Poverty rates in nonmetropolitan areas are 14.6 percent, compared with 11.8 percent in metropolitan areas (U.S. Census Bureau, 2003). Thus, we must build

NEW DIRECTIONS FOR COMMUNITY COLLEGES, no. 137, Spring 2007 © 2007 Wiley Periodicals, Inc.
Published online in Wiley InterScience (www.interscience.wiley.com) • DOI: 10.1002/cc.266

public policies with appropriate resources to address these differences, and strategically connect educational opportunities to community economic development. This chapter offers an overview of the realities of rural education, suggests needed research and policy analysis, and discusses possible strategies for addressing the challenges of the rural differential.

A Snapshot of the Rural Economy

Although some of rural America appears to be prospering, many areas are at increasing risk of economic decline, and others remain mired in persistent poverty. The rural middle class is shrinking, and young families, many of whom would like to stay near home, are leaving to find better jobs. Rural America may become "the involuntary home of the poor and the chosen home of the pleasure seekers, producing a rural ghetto and a rural playground" (Stauber, 2001, p. 36).

In addition, country stores and family farms continue to become fewer and larger. Manufacturing employment continues to slide. Globalization is driving a continuing consolidation in both agriculture and manufacturing. Unfortunately, the major public sector investments in rural economic development continue to be agricultural commodity subsidies and business tax incentives to lure large-scale manufacturing plants. The disconnect between these trends and rural public policy can be cast as a "perfect storm" or a "rural tipping point" (Fluharty, 2004, p. 2).

If the perfect storm metaphor is apt, then one particular group of counties is located in the eye of the storm. Three hundred and eighty-six counties across our nation are classified as "persistent poverty counties" (U.S. Department of Agriculture, 2004). In these counties, the poverty rate was at least 20 percent between 1970 and 2000. The majority of these counties (240, or 88 percent) are nonmetropolitan. Poverty is particularly pervasive among rural racial and ethnic minorities—Hispanics, African Americans, and Native Americans. As U.S. Department of Agriculture Undersecretary for Rural Development Tom Dorr has stated, what rural America needs is "viable businesses, self-sustaining communities, and young families eager to build a future" (Dorr, 2006, p. 4). How can rural community colleges more effectively respond to these needs?

The Rural Community College Response

If rural colleges and rural communities share a common destiny, then mutual engagement around strategies for building sustainable communities is essential. Community colleges excel in providing access to education, and were founded with the additional mission of supporting community needs (Cohen and Brawer, 2003). Moreover, if community colleges have a parallel responsibility to create opportunities that will keep those being educated in the community, connectivity between the college and community is required.

However, achieving this connection is difficult. The former CEO of the American Association of Community Colleges, David Pierce, got it right when he said: "The work of community revitalization is uncertain, and afflicted by the very fragmentation that we seek to correct" (Pierce, 1996, p. 4). Much of the uncertainty affecting the community college's community-building work is created by policies that treat institutions as if they were all essentially alike, no matter their context or location. Yet we know that geography and culture matter. Size and scale are crucial. Local social, political, and economic conditions impair or enable sustainability. In short, place matters.

In a special report addressing the challenges of how community colleges can contribute to their state's community and economic vitality, Rubin and others (2005) suggest five strategic imperatives for Mississippi's rural community colleges: (1) build human capital; (2) nurture social capital and strong, healthy communities; (3) work regionally; (4) find a competitive niche; and (5) promote a culture of entrepreneurship. Although noting that many other institutions or agencies may also employ one or more of these strategies, the authors assert that "the community college mission encompasses all five areas" (Rubin and others, 2005, p. 1). However, this study also noted that despite many local initiatives and broad support for community college engagement in community and economic development, "this aspect of the community college mission is largely unfunded" (p. 2).

The Rural Disadvantage in Federal Funding

Current federal funding policy inadvertently, but significantly, disadvantages the areas served by rural community colleges. *The Consolidated Federal Funds Report* for 2001, the most recently reported data on U.S. government expenditures by program and county, shows that the federal government returned $6,131 on a per capita basis to urban areas while returning only $6,020 to rural areas. This results in an almost $5.5 billion annual federal disadvantage to rural areas (Fluharty, 2006).

In 2001, direct payments to individuals, as a percent of all federal funds per capita, were 50.5 percent in metropolitan areas and 63.9 percent in non-metropolitan America (Reeder and Calhoun, 2002). This 13 percent differential in federal funding between rural and urban areas greatly affects the community capacity and infrastructure, and hinders rural communities' ability to strengthen their economies (Fluharty, 2006). In other words, resources directed to individuals in rural settings are greater per capita than in urban areas. This attenuates the residual per capita resources available for rural community infrastructure development. Individuals may be advantaged by federal funding policy in the short term, but in the long term rural communities are disadvantaged.

NEW DIRECTIONS FOR COMMUNITY COLLEGES • DOI: 10.1002/cc

With each passing year, these differences in payments further disadvantage rural jurisdictions and organizations, and they are forced to compete with their metropolitan counterparts on an increasingly uneven playing field without the benefit of the professional staff, technical assistance, and planning resources that this funding secures.

One reason why this funding differential exists is that metropolitan statistical areas have a "place entitlement" that allows them to collect community development block grants from the federal government. These funds are available each year, which allows for multiyear capital and program planning, and multiyear cross-sector capacity building. However, rural towns and cities with populations of less than fifty thousand and counties with populations of less than two hundred thousand must compete with one another for smaller, state-administered community development block grants, which are neither guaranteed nor provide multiyear funding.

These funding disadvantages are additive. Each year between 1994 and 2001, the federal government spent two to five times more, per capita, on urban than rural community development, and one-third as much on community resources in rural areas (W. K. Kellogg Foundation, 2004). Per capita spending on community resources in 2001 was $286 per person less in rural areas than in urban America—a $14.1 billion disadvantage, based on 2003 metropolitan classifications of the 2000 census population (U.S. Department of Agriculture, 2004).

Foundation and Corporate Grant-Making Gaps

The rural federal funding disadvantage is exacerbated by an equally uneven commitment to rural community and economic development by our nation's foundations and corporate grant makers. The National Committee for Responsive Philanthropy (2004) notes that of the $30 billion distributed annually by America's foundations, only $100.5 million was committed to rural development. Indeed, of the 65,000 active grant-making foundations in the United States, only 184 engaged in rural grant making. About 20 foundations accounted for 80 percent of this total, and 2 foundations, the W. K. Kellogg Foundation and the Ford Foundation, constituted 42 percent. The latter foundations' significant rural community and economic development commitment is commendable. However, most grant-making foundations in the United States have not seriously addressed the development needs of organizations serving rural populations.

According to the National Committee for Responsive Philanthropy (2004), the same rural differential is also evident in corporate philanthropy. Although total corporate grant making in the United States amounts to $12 billion annually, a "2000 study of the 124 Fortune 500 corporations found that corporate grant making for rural, racial/ethnic organizations amounted to 1 percent of their total racial/ethnic grant making" (National Committee for Responsive Philanthropy, 2004, p. 18). In total, "corporate grant making for rural groups constituted seven-tenths of 1 percent of the grant dollars awarded by the 124 surveyed corporations for racial/ethnic giving. . . . Rural organizations received only 153 of the 10,905 grants made, approximately 1.4 percent of all grants" (p. 18).

Accessing Resources: Another Hill to Climb

For rural community colleges, the difficulties of accessing these resources multiplies the challenges of institutional and community development. Rural colleges, like rural governmental jurisdictions, tend to have small staffs with multiple responsibilities. Simply tracking known government and philanthropic programs is beyond the capacity of many colleges and communities. With limited, if any, research staff, grant writers, technical assistance resources, or economic analysis capacity, these governmental jurisdictions and colleges are profoundly disadvantaged.

Furthermore, many of these programs encourage competition among institutions rather than collaborations that might allow colleges or communities to gain scale by pulling together in regional development. Isolated by geography and culturally conditioned to compete with one another, rural institutions have difficulty in building a critical population mass that is attractive to major funding interests, public or private. Competing for limited resources with limited staff is an additional disadvantage for small rural community colleges.

Funding the Mission

Rural community college leaders understand that educational and economic opportunity are parallel pathways that can lead to sustainable communities and colleges. They also know that strengthening rural community colleges' capacity to thrive as effective, comprehensive postsecondary institutions enables them to serve as catalysts for community and economic development. A widely accepted, comprehensive view of the community college mission "is to provide postsecondary programs and services that lead to stronger, more vital communities" (Vaughn, 2000, p. 3). In practice, this mission comprises many missions or functions, each of which is funded to varying degrees. The traditional missions of the community college are transfer, general education, and technical education (Katsinas, Alexander, and Opp, 2003). State funds to support these missions are usually allocated by credit-based formulas that focus on full-time equivalent enrollments in transfer and occupational programs. Student services, instructional support, and institutional operations are usually considered in creating these funding formulas.

However, the adequacy of state support—the primary funding stream for public community colleges—is a big issue for all community colleges. During the past twenty years, state support for community colleges has declined or shifted. Students are paying a larger share of instruction costs, while states are contributing less (Roessler, Katsinas, and Hardy, 2005). Furthermore, in rural areas of states that provide local tax support for community colleges, declining populations and eroding economies translate into declining tax assessments and revenues. Thus, adequacy of state and local support, an issue for all community colleges, is especially acute in rural community colleges.

For rural community colleges, equity is a major concern. Funding formulas that do not recognize the higher per-student operating costs of small colleges clearly disadvantage rural institutions. Declining state support and rising student tuition make conversations about equitable distribution of resources more difficult. However, there are a variety of ways to address the issue of scale-related equity. One way would be to change funding formulas in a state or provide special funding for rural community colleges so that they can reach parity with their urban and suburban counterparts. Because achieving and maintaining equity among all colleges must occur state by state, state directors and state association officers are key leaders in framing equity conversations. Rural colleges have a vital interest in ensuring that issues of equity and adequacy are addressed.

Resources for the Unfunded Community Development Mission

Most state community college systems acknowledge a variety of community and economic development–related missions. Katsinas, Alexander, and Opp (2003) identify four: industry training, developmental education, community service, and continuing education. Funding for these functions varies greatly among the states.

Because credit hours are widely accepted and readily counted, resources tend to flow toward activities that produce credits. In functional areas such as workforce development, measures of performance or outputs are less well-defined. Thus, workforce development or industry training funding tends to be additive, episodic, and unstable (Pugh, 2005).

Rural community college work in community and economic development activities is also usually project-specific, locally initiated, regionally focused, and unrecognized in state funding plans. Therefore, the results are usually anecdotally described projects and activities, frequently involving multiple partners and a variety of public and private funding sources. These programs also tend to be place-specific. For example, Alabama Southern Community College, located in the hometown of Harper Lee, author of *To Kill a Mockingbird,* has led the development of a state literary festival engaging many partners. In Wesson, Mississippi, Copiah-Lincoln Community College helped link the development of a college-owned golf course to community residential development. These are not programmatically funded activities but are place-focused community economic development activities with multiple partners. Exemplary programs such as these exist, but in isolation from one another.

Barnett and others (2003) cite a broad range of community and economic development activities of this type. However, Rubin describes these activities as "largely unfunded" (Rubin and others, 2005, p. 2). Typically, state support systems require the rural community college to choose between traditionally funded, mission-related activities that have a "college" focus or unfunded, mission-related activities that have a "community" focus. Most rural community colleges choose to do both. The impact of sporadic funding for rural community colleges means that community events constantly run the risk of not occurring. The potential for lack of funding often means that volunteers or other groups bear an increased burden to make sure these programs are provided to the community. The uncertainty surrounding community programming means that the populations most in need of services may not have access.

The Path Ahead

Rural America desperately needs a clearer connection between college and community. The shared futures of rural colleges and rural communities require a rethinking and realignment of the rural college mission as well as new policy frameworks that support both community colleges and rural community development.

Several issues remain to be addressed. These include discovering the answers to the following questions: How can place and culture contribute to building sustainable rural communities? How can we advance responsiveness and flexibility as key values in executing the community college mission? Are we ready to have real conversations about the community dimension of these institutions? Are we ready to expand measures of college success to include community as well as college viability? Although these are issues to be addressed by researchers, policymakers, and community college advocates, many rural community colleges are engaged daily in pioneering additional examples of creating opportunities in place (Barnett and others, 2003).

References

Barnett, L., and others. *Opportunities in Place: National Assessment of the Rural Community College Initiative.* Washington, D.C.: Community College Press, 2003.

Carnegie Foundation for the Advancement of Teaching. *The Carnegie Classification of Institutions of Higher Education.* Stanford, Calif.: Carnegie Foundation for the Advancement of Teaching, 2006. http://www.carnegiefoundation.org/classifications/. Accessed Nov. 20, 2006.

Cohen, A. M., and Brawer, F. B. *The American Community College.* (4th ed.) San Francisco: Jossey-Bass, 2003.

Dorr, T. *Remarks: AG Outlook Forum/Rural Development Track.* Washington, D.C.: U.S. Department of Agriculture, Office of Rural Development, 2006.

Fluharty, C. W. "New Approaches to Rural Policy: Affirming the Role of Rural Community Colleges." Paper presented at the annual conference of the Rural Community College Alliance, Myrtle Beach, S.C., Oct. 4, 2004.

Fluharty, C. W. "Testimony Before the U.S. House of Representatives, House Committee on Agriculture, Subcommittee on Conservation, Credit, Rural Development and Research." Washington, D.C., Mar. 30, 2006.

Hardy, D. E., and Katsinas, S. G. "Using Community College Classifications in Research: From Conceptual Model to Useful Tool." *Community College Journal of Research and Practice,* 2006, *30,* 339–358.

Katsinas, S., Alexander, K., and Opp, R. D. *Preserving Access with Excellence: Financing for Rural Community Colleges.* Rural Community College Initiative Policy Paper. Chapel Hill, N.C.: MDC, Inc., 2003.

Miller, K. K., and Rowley, T. D. *Rural Poverty and Rural Urban Income Gaps: A Troubling Snapshot of the "Prosperous" 1990s.* Columbia, Mo.: Rural Policy Research Institute, 2002.

National Committee for Responsive Philanthropy. *State of Philanthropy, 2004.* Washington, D.C.: National Committee for Responsive Philanthropy, 2004.

Pierce, D. "Building Communities on Firm Foundations." Paper presented at the W. K. Kellogg Foundation Rural Conference at the annual conference of the American Association of Community Colleges, Battle Creek, Mich., June 1996.

Pugh, J. "An Exploration of Advantages Associated with Stable Funding for State-Supported Workforce Education as an Impetus for Change in Mississippi's Funding of Workforce Education." Unpublished doctoral dissertation, Mississippi State University, 2005.

Reeder, R. J., and Calhoun, S. J. "Federal Funds in Rural America: Payments Vary by Region and Type of County." *Rural America,* 2002, *17*(3), 1–3.

Roessler, B. C., Katsinas, S., and Hardy, D. *The Downward Spiral of State Funding for Community Colleges.* Policy Brief for the MidSouth Partnership for Rural Community Colleges. Meridian, Miss.: Rural Community College Alliance, 2005.

Rubin, S., and others. "Invigorating Rural Economies: The Rural Development Mission of Mississippi's Community Colleges." Special Report of the MidSouth Partnership for Rural Community Colleges No. PSR-05–2. Meridian, Miss.: MidSouth Partnership for Rural Community Colleges, 2005.

Stauber, K. "Why Invest in Rural America and How? A Critical Public Policy Question for the 21st Century." *Economic Review, Federal Reserve Bank of Kansas City,* 2001, *86*(2), 33–63.

U.S. Census Bureau. *United States Summary 2000: Summary Social, Economic, and Housing Characteristics.* Washington, D.C.: U.S. Census Bureau, 2003. (PHC 2–1)

U.S. Department of Agriculture. *Rural Poverty at a Glance.* Rural Development Research Report No. 100, Economic Research Service. Washington, D.C.: U.S. Department of Agriculture, 2004.

Vaughan, G. *The Community College Story.* (2nd ed.) Washington, D.C.: Community College Press, 2000.

W. K. Kellogg Foundation. *Mapping Rural Entrepreneurship.* Battle Creek, Mich.: W. K. Kellogg Foundation, Corporation for Enterprise Development, 2004.

CHARLES FLUHARTY *is director of the Rural Policy Research Institute and associate director of the Truman School of Public Affairs, University of Missouri-Columbia.*

BILL SCAGGS *is executive director of the Rural Community College Alliance.*

3

This chapter describes how rural community colleges use continuing education and other noncredit activities to provide key services to their surrounding communities that aid in creating group identity and engagement in the larger community.

Connecting Rural Community Colleges to Their Communities

Michael T. Miller, Daniel B. Kissinger

Rural America accounts for 85 percent of the nation's geography but only 15 percent of its population. This segment of the population is characterized as underperforming in bachelor's degree attainment, having higher poverty rates and fewer opportunities for advancement, and in many areas, experiencing sustained economic depression. Yet over forty-five million Americans continue to choose rural living, often citing reasons such as increased feelings of personal safety, preserving family heritage and tradition, and the opportunity to lead a simpler life (Annie E. Casey Foundation, 2004).

Key to a rural community's survival and success is a social engine that drives the community's economy and serves as a foundation for group identity formation and engagement. Social engines can be businesses, offices, agencies, schools, or traditions that bring a community together and provide the locus for group identity formation. However, in many rural communities, particularly those that are farm-based, there are few, if any, social engines. Historically, the social engine that drives a rural community's identity and functioning is something with the size and economic strength or influence to meaningfully engage the community. With a history of serving a community's educational needs and bringing statewide resources and opportunities to rural America, rural community colleges often serve as the cultural and community center for their communities. This chapter examines community identification and rural community colleges' interactions

with and influences on their communities and community members through leisure education programs, cultural enrichment programs, economic development programs, and educational opportunities. The chapter concludes with a discussion of the power of these influences to assist in community members' identity development.

Community Identification

For more than half a century there has been a struggle to define and adapt the concept of community to something other than a physical space or a governmentally defined location, such as a township or village. As Fordham (1956) argued fifty years ago, the concept of community relies on the idea that individuals interact on a social level and depend on one another, and this process of interaction takes place regardless of physical location. From this perspective, a community is both a place and a process that involves symbolic, cultural, and personal interaction.

Levy (1966) outlined four core elements of community identity. First, all communities have common aspects, such as role differentiation (age, generation, sex), solidarity, and economic and political allocation. Second, all communities have common organizations, such as families, government bodies, and predominantly economically oriented organizations. Third, communities have an underlying set of clustered relationships (neighborhoods) and specialized sets of relationship aspects (such as churches and social organizations). Finally, communities have common problems related to socialization, economic allocation, political stability, and the discrepancy between ideal and actual structures.

More recently, Bushy (2000) defined the social elements unique to rural communities, finding that residents are often related or acquainted. They have interactions with other community members that are less formal and more face-to-face, have a general preference for interacting with local individuals and mistrust outsiders, and find that it is often difficult to maintain anonymity. The primary centers of socialization and interaction in rural communities tend to be clustered in or near local schools, colleges, and churches. Bushy compared this environment to urban centers where there is less familiarity among residents, social interactions tend to be more formal, and there is a wider array of designated places for socialization, business, and recreation.

The primary implication of these community identification concepts for rural community colleges is that the activities of colleges are scrutinized more and felt more intensely in rural communities than in urban centers. Rural community college activities have the potential to affect the entire community in both intended and unintended ways, and it is this ripple effect from program development and execution that is of particular interest to those working in rural revitalization.

NEW DIRECTIONS FOR COMMUNITY COLLEGES • DOI: 10.1002/cc

The Influence of Rural Community Colleges

Rural colleges involve and influence the activities, status, and identity of their communities through four noncredit programs in particular: leisure education, cultural enrichment, economic development, and continuing education. Each of these four program areas is discussed here, first to examine how rural community colleges provide that function, and then to explore how doing so provides interaction with a community and its members. For each program area, how the rural community college can build, change, or influence a community member's sense of self and identity is discussed. This fundamental idea of the community college impact on a community has been a central and growing tenet in the work of the MidSouth Partnership for Community Colleges, which works with these institutions to improve the quality of rural citizens' lives.

The following discussion is predicated on several controlling ideas about identity development and the exploration of life transitions (Cass, 1979; Cross, 1971; Downing and Roush, 1985; Erikson, 1959, 1980; Josselson, 1987; Marcia, 1966). Erikson and Josselson's models of identity development are used as a foundation to explore identity development among community members in rural settings that host rural community colleges.

Leisure Education. In rural communities, the community college can meet the unique learning needs of the community. Although this is true of many community colleges, it is particularly true in rural communities where the college is often the only easily accessible option for residents. Leisure education programs offered by community colleges grew from a desire to be responsive to the unique needs of their communities. Indeed, college leaders realized that success in continuing funding and the fulfillment of their unique institutional mission was tied closely to the concept of engaging community members in a variety of programs throughout their life span. Leisure education programs range from study-travel programs (both domestic and international) to physical fitness classes for senior citizens. For instance, at Bevill State Community College in Alabama, summer sports camps are offered to meet the needs of local youth and at the same time bring future generations of college students to the campus at an early age. Because of these camps, many students who would not otherwise consider postsecondary education are exposed to the idea of college (Miller and Tuttle, 2006).

In addition, leisure education programs provide an organized structure for continued and recreational learning. In many rural communities, parks and recreation programs operate on limited budgets, and community colleges (either intentionally or not) offer complementary programming. Some community college facilities are used for activities such as classes, youth swimming lessons, a community swimming pool, a partner for local nursing home training, and organized card or game clubs.

NEW DIRECTIONS FOR COMMUNITY COLLEGES • DOI: 10.1002/cc

The broad range of leisure education programs that community colleges offer presents a variety of opportunities for community members to change their frame of thinking about themselves. Most of these programs have unintended psychological and social outcomes. For example, a leisure sports program that involves winning and losing has implications for how the participating individuals see themselves and how they view competition. Some self-improvement programs such as weight loss, art, or sports classes can help individuals think of themselves in different ways than when they begin the program. Individuals often participate in a leisure program in response to some internal or external crisis, and this participation may lead to a different resolution and subsequently change an individual's self-concept and identity. For example, participation in a weight control or nutrition program at a rural community college might be in response to increased feelings of inadequacy or a failure in some personal relationship. The resultant change may also be less intentional. For example, when an individual sits next to someone of a different ethnicity in class or participates in programs that provide exposure to world differences, it may result in a changed global perspective; similarly, accomplishing an activity or task may lead to greater self-confidence and self-awareness. In these kinds of activities, self-identity is not the aim of the instruction but rather an unintended by-product of the educational experience. Other types of social interactions that might arise from leisure programming are as basic as using a community health complex for leisure swimming or exercise, as individuals do at John A. Logan Community College in southern Illinois. In this setting, the interaction that results from using this facility can be an impetus for social networking outside of traditional or familial boundaries and can result in self-challenging thinking about relationships. Thus, rural community colleges both link the college with the community and link the individuals in the community. These two layers of linkages ultimately help build community, and they are unique to rural areas in which the variety of social engines or group-building bodies is limited.

Cultural Enrichment. As indicated in a recent Annie E. Casey Foundation (2004) report, many rural communities pride themselves on offering a quality of life that stresses commitment to family, heritage, tradition, and safety. A key component of this professed lifestyle is a commitment to cultural activities that expand the mind, challenge traditional thinking, and reflect the diversity, complexity, and beauty of the world and human nature. Rural community colleges are key providers in expanding cultural awareness in their communities. North Arkansas Community College (NACC), for example, provides a summer concert series, bringing symphonies and culturally diverse music to its campus in the small town of Harrison. These concerts, as well as lectures and visiting speakers throughout the year, are not profit-making activities and rarely are put on as course-related incentives for students. Rather, these activities are intended to add to the quality of life of the township. The president of NACC indicated that his vision for such activities was to place the college at the center of the town's activities—

not for the glory of the college but rather to meet the needs of the community, and at times to challenge community members to think differently about the world around them (Miller and Tuttle, 2006).

The impact these cultural activities have on their communities is substantial. They bring a sense of culture and exposure to different ways of thinking to rural community members who would not otherwise have access to such programs. As well, cultural activities can ease individuals into a state of role confusion that can lead to different identity resolutions. As an individual's identity goes through various stages of development, participation in activities sponsored by rural community colleges can lead to temporary, continuous, or even permanent changes. For example, a person might learn to view foreigners in a different light or even imagine visiting or living in another part of the world. In addition, exposure to different types of people can lead community members to confront their attitudes about race or ethnicity, and can force individuals—even adults—into stages of identity crisis that lead to alternative resolutions.

Economic Development. Perhaps the most popular rural community college economic activities involve workforce development and short-term contract training and retraining programs for business and industry. In largely rural states such as Nebraska and Mississippi, state-funded research and development units have worked with community colleges to broker state department of labor, economic development, and social services funding to help businesses prosper in otherwise challenging locations. These training activities have historically included adult basic literacy instruction, employee certification to use certain machinery, training in International Standards Organization (ISO) certification, and displaced worker training or retraining. Contract training programs, often subsidized by the state and offered by many community colleges, deal with changes to production processes or methods of manufacturing. In the 1990s, for example, computer-automated design (CAD) and computer-assisted machinery (CAM) instruction were popular contract training areas, and community colleges helped frontline workers deal with advances in production automation. Rural community colleges also offer support for small business development, often providing the resources necessary for incubating a business idea, assisting in state and federal paperwork or loan applications, and even providing initial office space for new small businesses. East Mississippi Community College, which has multiple campuses, is one example of an institution that provides this type of service, working on the premise that as the college grows and changes to be responsive to the society, the entire town and region benefit.

However, the preparation and retraining of the labor force can also result in changing visions of self-identity. Through workforce preparation, for example, individuals might begin to envision a different occupation or quality of life. Through training exercises, workers might begin to think about pursuing careers in management, those working in service or manufacturing jobs might see themselves in different kinds of work, and those seeking diplomas or certificates might begin to see themselves earning associate or bachelor's degrees. The college, through its training and retraining programs, can be a catalyst that pushes an individual into some state of crisis that leads to a different identity resolution. This is particularly important in the many rural areas that have experienced sustained economic depression, because the community college can help local residents improve their quality of life. Rural colleges also have the ability to reinforce local lifestyle and labor opportunities, adding to the community's ability to continue rural life and protect familial heritage while at the same time providing opportunities for outmigration to other rural locales or to urban areas.

Educational Opportunities. Most community colleges, whether rural, urban, or suburban, provide relatively open access. This open door approach to higher education allows a broad spectrum of individuals to enroll in community college courses and programs, bringing a student body to campus that has a diverse array of unique characteristics, cultures, backgrounds, assumptions, and beliefs. Such is the case in Newton County, Mississippi, where the secondary school consists of a largely white private academy and a largely African American public high school. Both populations merge in East Central Community College (ECCC) in Decatur, and the racial integration provides an opportunity for students to explore one another's culture, differences, and similarities. ECCC's diverse enrollment has been well received and students have consistently reported having positive feelings and experiences with an increased sense of diversity in their classes and on campus (Miller and Tuttle, 2006).

Like economic development training, exposure to different people and ideas can lead to individuals challenging their previously predetermined life expectations. Thus, as they take classes and see themselves in different settings, they learn to imagine other life outcomes. For example, traditional college-age students enrolling in a two-year college typically experience role confusion and crisis related to intimacy and isolation (Erikson, 1980). This key developmental crisis involves the struggle to formulate positive, egalitarian relationships, and successful resolution is illustrated by the ability to establish critical social relationships. Enrollment in a community college provides the social interaction that is the primary medium for age-appropriate identity formation. This includes, for example, challenging thinking about other social groups, as was the case at ECCC (Miller and Tuttle, 2006). Nontraditional-age college students challenge preexisting biases or confront topics ranging from racial stereotyping to occupational choices.

Discussion and Conclusion

The colleges connecting with their communities that were highlighted in this chapter illustrate the rural community college's power to help build its community and its ability to help frame how community members see themselves. Many institutions, like Lewis and Clark Community College in

Godfrey, Illinois, include providing cultural, civic, and professional activities as part of their mission statement, while others are driven by presidential or institutional leadership initiatives to connect with their communities. In the process, these institutions meet their unique community needs while also anticipating future needs and attempting to broaden community awareness. Whether community colleges provide health centers, community education, or even assistance in preparing income tax reports, these institutions offer unique opportunities to address the economic and social issues present in rural America.

College administrators in rural settings will find it helpful to explore the activities offered by North Arkansas Community College and Bevill State Community College in Alabama, both of which are actively engaged in their communities' livelihood. Bevill State Community College, for example, provides a broad range of opportunities for students to compete in sports, and does so for a variety of reasons, including to engage the community in the activities of the college, to bring community members together in a social setting, to offer opportunities for local residents to pursue sports at the college level, and to offer an additional economic activity for the community.

College leaders must look to their community to identify both its immediate and future needs, and then respond accordingly. These needs might be economic or cultural, and responses need to be planned in such a way that they complement the activities provided by other public agencies. This may be particularly difficult if colleges increasingly build their academic transfer function and move further away from their roots in job training, vocational education, and responding to immediate local community needs.

Along with accurately conceptualizing and responding to changing institutional and cultural dynamics, colleges must face developmental challenges across the broader rural spectrum. This chapter described a range of activities that community colleges can sponsor to facilitate identity development and to enhance or challenge "a firm and secure sense of self" (Sternberg and Williams, 2002, p. 85). These are especially important because, in many instances, community colleges are critical to the financial and cultural economies of their communities. Thus, by providing programs and activities that bridge the educational, social, leisure, and vocational needs of their communities, colleges extend their reach outside of the academic realm and serve as a medium for facilitating identity development (Josselson, 1987; Marcia, 1966).

Community college collaboration with other rural agencies is also important for community development. College administrators will find that providing a broad range of programs that connect with other social agencies and industries can positively affect the quality of life in a community through the development of self-assurance and identity resolution for community members. Rural community colleges are among the few social agencies that can be a conduit for state funding to rural areas, can provide programs and activities that reach all segments of a community, and can affect both future and immediate community needs. This means that colleges have a rare opportunity to help solve the problems that continue to challenge many rural areas and that their leaders can help sustain rural America in the twenty-first century.

References

Annie E. Casey Foundation. *The High Cost of Being Poor: What It Takes for Low-Income Families to Get By and Get Ahead in Rural America.* Baltimore: Annie E. Casey Foundation, 2004.

Bushy, A. *Orientation to Nursing in the Rural Community.* Thousand Oaks, Calif.: Sage, 2000.

Cass, V. C. "Homosexual Identity Formation: A Theoretical Model." *Journal of Homosexuality,* 1979, *4,* 219–235.

Cross, W. E. "The Negro-to-Black Conversion Experience: Toward a Psychology of Black Liberation." *Black World,* 1971, *20,* 13–27.

Downing, N. E., and Roush, K. L. "From Passive Acceptance to Active Commitment: A Model of Feminist Identity Development for Women." *Counseling Psychologist,* 1985, *13*(9), 695–709.

Erikson, E. H. "Identity and the Life Cycle." *Psychological Issues,* 1959, *1*(1), 1–71.

Erikson, E. H. *Identity and the Life Cycle.* (2nd ed.) New York: Norton, 1980.

Fordham, J. B. *A Larger Concept of Community.* Baton Rouge: Louisiana State University Press, 1956.

Josselson, R. *Finding Herself: Pathways to Identity Development in Women.* San Francisco: Jossey-Bass, 1987.

Levy, M. J. *Modernization and the Structure of Societies.* Princeton, N.J.: Princeton University Press, 1966.

Marcia, J. "Development and Validation of Ego Identity Status." *Journal of Personality and Social Psychology,* 1966, *3,* 551–558.

Miller, M. T., and Tuttle, C. C. "How Rural Community Colleges Develop Their Communities and the People Who Live in Them." Meridian, Miss.: MidSouth Partnership for Rural Community Colleges, 2006.

Sternberg, R. J., and Williams, W. M. *Educational Psychology.* Needham Heights, Mass.: Allyn & Bacon, 2002.

MICHAEL T. MILLER *is professor of higher education at the University of Arkansas.*

DANIEL B. KISSINGER *is assistant professor in counselor education at the University of Arkansas.*

4

Rural community college presidential job advertisements that focus on geography, politics, and culture can improve the likelihood of a good fit between the senior leader and the institution.

"Ruralizing" Presidential Job Advertisements

Jay Leist

Community college presidential job advertisements often reflect a "one-size-fits-all" mentality. Regardless of the institutional setting (rural, urban, or suburban), these want ads routinely contain a universal set of professional qualities. Besides reinforcing the notion that all community colleges are homogenous, this phenomenon can result in an advertisement focused more on personal attributes than organizational issues and challenges. More importantly, the lack of specificity can prevent a good fit—in other words, matching the professional qualities of a candidate with the needs of the hiring institution (Bumpas, 1998).

Rural, urban, and suburban two-year institutions are far from a homogenous group (Katsinas, 1996, 2003). Significant differences exist between rural community colleges and their metropolitan counterparts, especially when it comes to mission, location, culture, and constituencies (Eller and others, 1999; Valadez and Killacky, 1995). Limited resources, geographic isolation, and a static economy are but three examples of the many concerns that rural community college presidents face (Morelli, 2002). From a leadership perspective, these differences—and the issues and challenges they create for the institutional leader—raise two interrelated questions: Do rural community college presidents require professional qualities markedly different from their urban and suburban peers? And if so, what qualities do rural leaders view as critical?

NEW DIRECTIONS FOR COMMUNITY COLLEGES, no. 137, Spring 2007 © 2007 Wiley Periodicals, Inc.
Published online in Wiley InterScience (www.interscience.wiley.com) • DOI: 10.1002/cc.268

This chapter showcases selected findings from a study (Leist, 2005) that examined the professional qualities of rural community college presidents and how well their traits and characteristics are mirrored in job advertisements. Advertisements appearing in a national periodical over five years led to the creation of a baseline template of qualities typically sought for rural community college presidents. Fifteen rural community college presidents critiqued the template and recommended revisions for "ruralizing" future want ads to better reflect the effects that mission, location, culture, and constituencies can have on this leadership position.

After a brief discussion about the unique issues and challenges that rural community colleges and their leaders face, this chapter offers a rationale for ruralizing presidential want ads. The baseline template depicts these concerns because it contains many of the deficiencies typically found in job advertisements. These problem areas will then serve as a springboard for suggesting a major revision to the baseline template—a process that uses rurality and the situational context of the institution to create advertisements that are both accurate and informative, and that maximize the potential for a good fit between a presidential candidate and a rural community college.

Are Rural Community Colleges Really Different?

Based on telephone interviews with fifteen rural community college presidents located in nine states, this section describes the unique challenges facing rural community colleges and their leaders, as well as the professional qualities necessary in a rural college leader. Participants in this study noted that geography, politics, and the culture of a rural area profoundly affect the daily operations of a rural institution and the activities of its president. Successfully addressing these factors requires more than a mere toolbox filled with universal leadership qualities; rural presidents (and to some degree, rural faculty) must possess special traits and characteristics because, as one participant noted, "Rurals are different."

Rural Geography. Many rural institutions are isolated from the bright-light attractions and conveniences of a major city. This can create problems in recruiting and retaining students, faculty, and staff because— as several respondents indicated—some people simply do not want to live in a "little bitty town." In addition, rural community college service areas often encompass thousands of square miles and include many small school districts. The fifteen presidents who participated in this study conceded that rural geography makes time management skills extremely important, because presidents spend much of each workweek traveling across their service area to establish and maintain contact with local power brokers and school superintendents.

These presidents indicated that farming and ranching were the economic mainstays of their service areas, and that many of their students were first-generation collegians supporting the family farm. Besides having arduous agricultural responsibilities, some of these rural students endure long commutes to campus (upwards of one hundred miles). The predominance of agriculture in a rural community college service area can also affect tax revenues. With so much of a sparsely populated area dedicated to farming and ranching, rural institutions collect fewer tuition dollars because of low enrollments, as well as fewer tax dollars because land used for agricultural purposes is typically assessed at a lower rate. However, although agriculture was the mainstay of the economy for these particular presidents, other rural areas have mining or tourism as industry bases.

The agricultural flavor of the service areas for the presidents interviewed in this study also led several to become more aware of issues affecting farming and ranching. One of these leaders established a dialogue with farmers to better understand their techniques for crop production. His newfound knowledge helped tailor several course offerings at the institution. Another president, already familiar with cattle ranching, routinely visited livestock producers to swap stories about the local agricultural economy and institutional happenings. One president even learned to ride a horse to show her awareness of and support for the local equestrian industry.

Rural Politics. Each president who participated in this study also criticized the baseline template for not amplifying two political concerns: funding and the ability to influence local constituents. These senior leaders felt that funding formulas favor larger, more urban institutions. Although the institutional tax base of a rural college often consists of a single county dominated by farmland, these fifteen presidents argued that their service areas encompassed multiple counties over which the college had no taxing authority, and this often forces rural community colleges to accomplish tasks similar to those of their peers but without the same level of resources. One example stemming from a state funding bias may be called the "shallow-staff syndrome." This malady, caused by a shortage of administrative staff, forces rural presidents to wear a variety of hats and become adept in numerous areas (for example, identifying residence hall maintenance concerns, conducting equity investigations and judicial matters, and handling complaints about cafeteria food and roommate assignments). Because urban and suburban institutions enjoy better funding, they can hire a larger staff to handle numerous mundane and time-consuming nonpresidential tasks.

Diversity has a profound influence on America's community colleges. Diversity, however, can—and routinely does—assume a different form in a rural setting. Rural communities have a diverse array of people from different social and economic backgrounds, and rural community college presidents must be able to move easily across all cultural levels. Bankers and shopkeepers, along with farmers, ranchers, and truck drivers—many of whom have never attended college—are often the local movers and shakers. Despite the influence these local leaders possess, rural community college presidents must routinely work hard to educate them about the complicated economic, political, and social issues affecting higher education.

NEW DIRECTIONS FOR COMMUNITY COLLEGES • DOI: 10.1002/cc

Rural Culture. Culture is the third significant factor differentiating rural community colleges from those in urban and suburban areas. Feedback from the fifteen presidents included in this study indicated that rural culture is the most important issue to consider when identifying potential rural college presidents and faculty. Although geography, politics, and culture also flavor urban and suburban arenas, it is the cultural mindsets and values of local constituents that make rural two-year institutions different. These often reflect a conservative belief system laden with traditions and expectations that can produce culture shock for someone thrust into the role of community college president—especially someone who does not have prior exposure to, or an awareness of, the inner workings of rural America.

One of these cultural mindsets concerns the role of the community college itself. Recognizing that the institution is directly tied to their quality of life, rural citizens expect the president to serve as a visible force in the community. This visibility requires a president to constantly take the pulse of the populace for new ideas, offer institutional program updates, and most importantly, listen. This visibility also comes with a price. All fifteen presidents who participated in this study stated that a rural presidency truly qualifies as a "24/7 lifestyle." Constituents expect them (and to a certain degree, their spouses) to always look presidential and be accessible. Trips to the grocery store, jaunts that should take only minutes, often become lengthy ventures. Constituents, on recognizing *their* president, frequently use the aisles and checkout lines as venues for lobbying about institutional issues. Geography, politics, and culture can obviously affect the efforts of a rural community college president. As such, these factors warrant amplification in job advertisements for this leadership position.

"Ruralizing" the Presidential Job Advertisement

Clearly, rural community colleges face issues and challenges markedly different from their urban and suburban brethren. Without a national strategy to fuel local economic development and improve their quality of life, rural communities have increasingly looked to their two-year institutions for answers. Rural residents have asked their community colleges to reach out to underserved populations and provide the much-needed direction to revitalize local and area economies, create and nurture local partnerships, and establish regional collaborations—all aimed at building a better future (Garza and Eller, 1998). Logically, presidential job advertisements for this type of institution should include the qualities that will best complement the mission, location, culture, and constituencies of the local environment.

However, advertisements for a chief executive officer (CEO) or presidential position have been criticized for what they say, and more importantly, for what they fail to say (Khurana, 2002). All too often, board members and other individuals involved in presidential selections have failed to consider the needs and environment of the organization *before* identifying the necessary professional qualities. Instead of focusing on the situational context of the search and how well a candidate's background matches it, many organizations measure a CEO's ability "entirely by individual attributes, with no reference to the particular challenges facing the firm" (Khurana, 2002, p. 97). This approach can lead to an advertisement dominated by a universal set of professional qualities (for example, "good leader," "good communicator") and other buzzwords (such as "proven motivator") that a successful president supposedly embodies. Unfortunately, although rural community colleges differ greatly from their urban and suburban counterparts and face many unique challenges, rural presidential job advertisements infrequently include anything more than these universal qualities and buzzwords, as the baseline template (presented in Figure 4.1 and described in more detail in the following section) illustrates.

The Baseline Template

This baseline template provides a point-in-time marketplace perspective of the professional qualities desired in a rural community college president. I created this template from ninety-five rural community college presidential job advertisements. The template lists the required and desired professional qualities contained in these want ads, based on their frequency of occurrence (see Figure 4.1). Except for subtle references to rural familiarity and regional cultural concerns, the baseline template fails to amplify any leadership issues and challenges that a rural community college president routinely confronts.

As Figure 4.1 illustrates, past experience as a college administrator is given much importance in rural community college presidential job advertisements. Interestingly, many institutions make little distinction about the level of higher education from which that experience comes. While the number of advertisements requiring or desiring community college administrator experience was nearly equal (twenty-one and nineteen, respectively), the requirement to have expertise from some institution of higher education (thirty-two advertisements) reinforced the notion that a universal set of professional qualities exists for this position.

Appearing in only twenty-five of the ninety-five advertisements, "collaborative and participatory leadership" seemed to lose its appeal as a required quality over the five-year period during which I analyzed advertisements. Two explanations might account for this reduced emphasis. First, over the past few years, governmental entities have increased their calls for greater accountability throughout American higher education. Some rural community colleges may have decided that requiring a president to have a collaborative and participatory style might hinder his or her accountability efforts. A second explanation for this diminished emphasis might be based on the community college's desire to obtain a large applicant pool by exposing as many individuals as possible to an advertisement

Figure 4.1. Baseline Template for a Presidential Job Advertisement

CENTRAL COMMUNITY COLLEGE

Anytown, USA

The board of trustees of Central Community College (CCC) invites applications and nominations for the position of president. Founded in 1955, CCC is a regionally accredited, comprehensive community college with an annualized FTE of 2,500 and a student population of 3,000. CCC offers 15 associate degrees and certificate programs.

The next president of Central Community College must have at least a master's degree (doctorate preferred) and should possess a history of demonstrated success as a community college (or other higher education) administrator at or above the dean level. The president is expected to reside in the college's service area.

The individual chosen to lead CCC will possess the following professional qualities and characteristics:

• A vision of and dedication to the philosophy and mission of the comprehensive community college • Keen oral and written communicative skills • Knowledge of funding processes • Experience as a fundraiser • Knowledge of governmental processes • Commitment to quality education • Sensitivity to diversity, cultural issues, and equal opportunity and treatment • Expertise in network building with local schools, economic and workforce development agencies, business and industry, hospitals, labor organizations, and other higher education institutions • Collaborative and participatory leadership style • Strong student orientation • Knowledge of academic transfer and career-technical programs • Strategic planning expertise • Strong interpersonal skills • Integrity • Team-building expertise • Positive personal image • Commitment to faculty and staff development • Understanding of technology • Understanding of the teaching and learning process • Experience with labor relations or collective bargaining • Familiarity with rural issues • Experience with facilities development • Experience with quality improvement • A sense of humor

CCC also desires the following professional qualities and characteristics in its next president:

• Community college (or other higher education) teaching experience • Sensitivity to the regional culture • Experience interacting with boards of trustees • Understanding of the temper of a college • Understanding of global issues • Experience with intercollegiate athletics • Experience with international recruiting • Understanding of the value of a dollar rather than limiting it by asking only for those with a collaborative style (Chambers, 2001).

The most surprising fact arising from the creation of the baseline template involves the apparent downplaying of an institution's rurality. Despite the educational, economic, and sociological challenges endemic to many rural areas, and the impact these factors can have on a president, only twenty-two of the ninety-five advertisements categorized the institution as rural. An even smaller number (eight of ninety-five) listed "familiarity with rural issues" as a required quality.

Two rationales might explain why rural community colleges would choose to downplay rurality in—or omit it from—their presidential job advertisements. First, downplaying or failing to mention rurality implies a degree of institutional wariness about developing a suitable applicant pool. By not mentioning their status, community colleges can reduce a reader's fixation on the issues and challenges associated with rural institutions—and, ideally, win over promising candidates who want to be a college president but are unsure of their willingness to live in a rural locale. Second, and more important, downplaying or omitting rurality can imply that an institution does not view its rural location as requiring a different set of leadership skills than urban or suburban colleges.

One other interesting finding is evident in the baseline template. Although a doctorate has been called a must-have quality for a community college president (Vaughan, 1989), a master's degree continued to serve as the minimum educational credential for a rural community college president. This may be because the isolated location of these institutions discourages individuals with a terminal degree from applying. Faced with the need to expand their applicant pools, rural community colleges may feel compelled to also consider candidates without a doctorate.

A Better Approach

Clearly, the qualities listed in a rural community college presidential job advertisement do not always mirror what is really required of these senior leaders. In particular, want ads routinely fail to increase the probability of a good fit between a president and a rural college and community. In their efforts to fill a presidential vacancy, rural institutions routinely structure their advertisements around a universal set of professional qualities. Although these qualities are widely accepted, they often fail to amplify the concept of rurality and the context in which the institution currently finds itself.

The fifteen presidents interviewed for this study recommended a number of revisions to the baseline template to ruralize future advertisements. These senior leaders also provided a list of challenges and opportunities that institutions might consider when identifying the specific qualities in an advertisement. I describe these challenges and opportunities, as well as a more accurate and informative presidential job advertisement, later in this section. First, however, let us look at what participants in this study agreed was one of the most important qualities for rural community college presidents: an ability to "tell the story."

Telling the Story. "Telling the story" exemplifies the skill rural presidents must possess to frame issues, sell plans, and engage various constituencies. In rural venues, telling the story means employing keen communicative skills to talk with constituents about what they want from their institution and the success stories in which the college has played a primary role. The ways in which rural presidents craft the story of their institution plays into the culture and history of the area and can be used as leverage for change.

Assimilation into the rural community is critical to the success of a rural community college president. In rural locales, the senior institutional leader is often placed on a pedestal. Possessing a terminal degree and a global perspective, earning one of the region's larger salaries, and being charged with moving the institution and the local area forward all make this person more than just a fixture at the top of an organizational chart. Shouldering this responsibility requires a president to learn about and appreciate every facet of the community. The role requires great passion, authenticity, energy, a sense of humor, and as several of the respondents emphasized, the ability to move the institution forward by molding it to the community—instead of the other way around. Applicants for the position of rural community college president must appreciate the cohesive bond that exists between an institution and the community.

Rural roots—or at least some exposure to the rural way of life—provide a distinct advantage in understanding this bond and the local culture. According to the participants in this study, having rural roots—though seldom listed in an advertisement—can offer a president a measure of credibility with constituents. Although someone from an urban or suburban setting may do well as the senior leader of a rural institution, a personal knowledge of—and comfort with—rural culture appears crucial to ensuring the likelihood of a good fit.

Rural community college presidential job advertisements also frequently fail to reveal the situational context of the institution (for example, the current status of the college, where the institution needs or wants to go, and what factors might affect its ability to get there). Most of the respondents agreed that applicants deserve an accurate picture of the status of and challenges faced by the institution. Including this snapshot in a job advertisement can offer applicants an understanding of what they will encounter upon assuming the position and whether they possess the necessary skills and drive to succeed in it.

To better understand the professional qualities needed by future rural community college presidents, I asked each respondent to consider the various challenges and opportunities associated with his or her position. As might be expected, they identified two areas affecting all sectors of American higher education—funding and the use of technology. More importantly, the fifteen presidents expressed concern about several challenges and opportunities endemic to rural locales: hiring and developing presidents who understand rurality, fighting for rural education, investing in and meeting the needs of the local populace, and telling the story. When properly framed, these concerns can serve as the basis for a more accurate and informative job advertisement for the position of rural community college president.

Creating More Accurate and Informative Advertisements. The first major revision to the baseline template involves the lead paragraphs (see Figure 4.2). Although beginning with the typical information found in most presidential job advertisements (for example, institutional age, student population, and so forth), these paragraphs should emphasize an institution's rurality. They should provide potential applicants with a better understanding of the geography of the area, as well as a degree of political information about the size of the college's service area, its economic and educational composition, and other institution-specific items.

More importantly, however, these lead paragraphs should stress the traditional bonds between the institution and its constituents, and the need to nurture this relationship by engaging, respecting, and embracing the culture. To enhance this nurturing effort, the lead sentence should suggest that an applicant have rural roots or previous rural community college experience. Although having this background may not guarantee success, nor its absence turn out to be a recipe for failure, many of the respondents in this study pointed to a genuine understanding of rural life as warranting special emphasis in future advertisements.

This showcasing of the mission, location, culture, and constituencies of the college serves as a springboard for the next major revision: a paragraph about the issues and challenges faced by the institution; in particular, its situational context. Two scenarios are used as examples (see again Figure 4.2). The first depicts a scenario not uncommon in many rural community colleges: declining enrollments. The second announces the forthcoming expansion into a new academic market by establishing a baccalaureate program in nursing.

The final revision to the baseline template involves identifying specific traits and characteristics that will best complement the rural nature of the institution and its situational context. This effort will require more than a simple reliance on a universal set of professional qualities. It will require serious introspection by the institution to determine its present condition, what problems it faces, and its priorities—and what professional qualities in a president will best support these concerns (Poston, 1997). This effort should also identify professional qualities that will assist a president in negotiating the political milieu of the local area. Examples might include the ability to tell the story, comfort with rural cultures and people from all walks of life, a willingness to constantly give of one's self for the greater good, and recognition that rural constituents want a leader to simultaneously improve their quality of life and safeguard their lifestyle.

New Directions for Community Colleges • DOI: 10.1002/cc

Figure 4.2. An Accurate and Informative Rural Presidential Job Advertisement

---

CENTRAL COMMUNITY COLLEGE

Anytown, USA

Central Community College (CCC) is seeking a president familiar with, dedicated to, and appreciative of rural values, and committed to enhancing the educational, economic, and cultural quality of life of the local residents. Founded in 1955, CCC is a comprehensive community college with an annualized FTE of 2,500 and a student population of 3,000; many are first-generation collegians. CCC offers 15 associate degrees and certificate programs and includes three residence halls.

The Cultural Setting

CCC is located in Anytown, USA (population 8,000), and is approximately 100 miles from the nearest metropolitan area. The economy of Anytown and the nine-county service area (covering 9,000 square miles) primarily depends on farming and ranching. This area includes seven independent school districts, all reliant on CCC for educational support. Constituents from diverse walks of life are proud of their conservative, small-town values; historical traditions; educational, cultural, and recreational activities; and close-knit relationship with the institution. CCC expects its next president to genuinely engage, respect, and embrace the local populace and its culture, while simultaneously looking for ways to ensure future regional prosperity. This presidency is a high-visibility, community pillar position, and its incumbent is expected to participate in community events and support local establishments.

Sample Situational Contexts

Situation 1: CCC has seen a steady decline in enrollments over the past three years. State universities have increasingly become the first choice of local students. These outmigrations have adversely affected the labor force of the regional economy. The next CCC president will be asked to reverse this decline by developing long-term solutions and by continuing to move the institution forward, while also enhancing the educational, economic, and cultural needs of the local citizens.

Situation 2: CCC recently obtained state approval to begin a four-year nursing degree program. At the state's request, CCC is trying to accelerate the start of this program to counteract future nursing shortages. The next CCC president will be expected to lead this program to fruition and continue to move the institution forward, while also enhancing the educational, economic, and cultural needs of the local citizens. The nursing program will require several major construction and space reallocation programs, coordination with state regulators and area hospitals, and is fueled, in part, by both federal grants and CCC benefactors.

Conclusion

Ruralizing presidential job advertisements may increase the probability of a good fit between a rural community college president and the institution. To realize this fit, future advertisements should amplify the concept of rurality and the situational context of the institution. As the available literature has repeatedly emphasized, the mission, location, culture, and constituencies of rural community colleges *are* different from their urban and suburban peers. Presidential advertisements need to showcase this difference by highlighting the rurality of the institution—its geography, its politics, its cultural flavor, and the expectations that constituents have for their senior leader.

Showcasing the situational context of the institution should be equally important. Presidential job advertisements should provide potential applicants with a thumbnail sketch of the current status of the organization. For example, why did the advertised vacancy occur? Was it because the incumbent leader is choosing to retire or because she wants to move on to bigger challenges? Is the institution looking for a president who can reverse recent declines in enrollment? Does the college need an experienced fundraiser to oversee a capital campaign, or someone adept at implementing baccalaureate programs?

This approach to ruralizing a community college presidential job advertisement is different from the norm. Although it downplays the importance of a universal set of professional qualities, it does not abandon them. Instead, the approach serves as a way to amplify the concept of rurality and encourages an institution to candidly tell the story of its people and its leadership issues, challenges, and opportunities. Emphasizing these critical factors can facilitate the good fit so desperately needed by rural community colleges and rural America. The process of developing the job advertisement also provides the search committee with an opportunity to be clear about their desires in a new leader.

References

Bumpas, R. K. "Factors That Affect the Selection of Community College Presidents." Unpublished doctoral dissertation, Texas A&M University, 1998.

Chambers, H. E. *Finding, Hiring, and Keeping Peak Performers.* Cambridge, Mass.: Perseus, 2001.

Eller, R., and others. *Rural Community College Initiative IV: Capacity for Leading Institutional and Community Change.* Report No. AACC-PB-99–3. Washington, D.C.: American Association of Community Colleges, 1999. (ED 432 332)

Garza, H., and Eller, R. D. "The Role of Rural Community Colleges in Expanding Access and Economic Development." In D. McGrath (ed.), *Creating and Benefiting from Institutional Collaboration: Models for Success.* New Directions for Community Colleges, no. 103. San Francisco: Jossey-Bass, 1998.

Katsinas, S. G. "Preparing Leaders for Diverse Institutional Settings." In J. C. Palmer and S. G. Katsinas (eds.), *Graduate and Continuing Education for Community College Leaders: What It Means Today.* New Directions for Community Colleges, no. 95. San Francisco: Jossey-Bass, 1996.

Katsinas, S. G. "Two-Year College Classifications Based on Institutional Control, Geography, Governance, and Size." In A. C. McCormick and R. D. Cox (eds.), *Classification Systems for Two-Year Colleges*. New Directions for Community Colleges, no. 122. San Francisco: Jossey-Bass, 2003.

Khurana, R. *Searching for the Corporate Savior: The Irrational Quest for Charismatic CEOs*. Princeton, N.J.: Princeton University Press, 2002.

Leist, J. E. "Exemplary Rural Community College Presidents: A Case Study of How Well Their Professional Qualities Mirror Job Advertisements." Unpublished doctoral dissertation, Texas Tech University, 2005.

Morelli, P. "Promoting Academic, Business, and Community Partnerships in Rural Areas." Paper presented at the annual meeting of the Rural Community College Association, Memphis, Oct. 2002. (ED 473 194)

Poston, M. E. "Presidential Search Committee Checklist." *Academe*, 1997, 83(5), 30–32.

Valadez, J. R., and Killacky, J. "Opening the Shutter." In J. Killacky and J. R. Valadez (eds.), *Portrait of the Rural Community College*. New Directions for Community Colleges, no. 90. San Francisco: Jossey-Bass, 1995.

Vaughan, G. B. *Leadership in Transition: The Community College Presidency*. New York: American Council on Education/Macmillan, 1989.

JAY LEIST is visiting assistant professor in the College of Education at Texas Tech University in Lubbock, Texas

5

This chapter describes a "grow-your-own" leader development program that emphasizes cross-disciplinary, multisector programs and activities that reinforce the community-building role of rural community, junior, and technical colleges.

Engaging Leaders as Builders of Sustainable Rural Communities: A Case Study

Molly M. Clark, Ed Davis

Over the last ten years, the challenge of building leadership capacity for America's community, technical, and junior colleges has received heightened attention (Shults, 2001). Vaughn and Weisman (1998) argue that there is "increased complexity in the presidency" (p. 17) and point out that community college leaders must understand and engage with a broad range of movements, organizations, and actors. They must understand and respond to economic globalization, profound changes in manufacturing and agriculture, continuing population shifts, persistent rural poverty, and a growing technological divide. Increasingly, the challenge for the rural community college leader is to engage deeply with the community to respond to these tides of change. This level of engagement calls for a systemic approach to thinking about the role rural colleges play in their communities. How rural leaders react to pressing changes is especially important because rural community colleges must serve as catalysts for economic renewal (Rubin and Autry, 1998).

This chapter describes the MidSouth Partnership for Rural Community Colleges (MSP), a regionally specific "grow-your-own" leadership development program that helps community college leaders build sustainable rural communities. The MSP was initiated in 1998 and is an ongoing collaboration of Alcorn State University, Mississippi State's John C. Stennis Institute

NEW DIRECTIONS FOR COMMUNITY COLLEGES, no. 137, Spring 2007 © 2007 Wiley Periodicals, Inc.
Published online in Wiley InterScience (www.interscience.wiley.com) • DOI: 10.1002/cc.269

of Government, and community colleges across the mid-South. Influenced and inspired by the Ford Foundation, funded by the Rural Community College Initiative (Barnett and others, 2003), the MSP addresses the challenge of building sustainable rural communities while renewing and expanding a diverse cadre of effective community college leaders. Key elements of the MSP leader development process include a weeklong retreat with follow-up programming, cross-disciplinary academic degree programs with a rural development emphasis, public policy analysis and doctoral dissertation research by practitioners, and systemic linkage to national rural and educational issues.

Coordination of these elements requires continuing formal and informal communication among all stakeholders and a commitment to supporting learning communities around leadership and community development. The biggest challenge to leader development is the creation of structures that support the continuous process of learning (Amey, 2005). The personal commitment of community and junior college presidents to the work of the MSP is the foundational strength of the grow-your-own leader approach. This chapter begins by first describing the MSP and its Community College Leadership (CCL) program. We then provide a review of critical links with a research support system and existing state and national rural policy organizations. The chapter concludes with a summary of lessons learned by the partnership that can guide readers interested in building their own leadership development program.

The MidSouth Community College Fellowship Program

The MidSouth Community College Fellowship Program (MCCFP), an intensive leadership orientation retreat, was established in 1994 with assistance from the Phil Hardin Foundation, a Mississippi philanthropic organization. Since 1995, participating colleges, the Mississippi State Board for Community and Junior Colleges, and the Lower Pearl River Valley Foundation have provided direct financial or staff support. Initially developed as a one-week leadership program, MCCFP has evolved into a yearlong educational program for current and past fellows. The MCCFP has proven to be a successful vehicle for engaging emerging leaders in an ongoing developmental process, encouraging university–community college collaboration, linking policy research to practitioner needs, and building cross-institutional, multidisciplinary, and cross-sector networks to support the next generation of community college leaders. Indeed, in June 2005 the Southern Growth Policies Board recognized the MSP as Regional Innovator of the Year (Bragg, 2002).

MSP fellows are nominated by the CEO of a community or junior college in the southeastern United States. Fellows have come from Alabama, Arkansas, Georgia, Louisiana, Kentucky, Mississippi, and North Carolina. The nomination process is seen as an opportunity to begin mentorship for future leadership positions in the college and the community. Nominees are usually employees of the nominating institution but may come from outside two-year colleges. Each year, most of Mississippi's community colleges and the Mississippi State Board for Community and Junior Colleges participate in the program. Twenty-five to thirty fellows are selected annually.

MCCFP initiates each class of fellows with a weeklong retreat, which includes training sessions on topics such as organizational and community change, conflict resolution, building consensus, the politics of education, and engaging diversity. Seasoned community college presidents and university faculty who specialize in education, rural sociology, economics, and political science serve as teachers and mentors. The retreats emphasize teamwork and networking.

During the week, all participants are introduced to a problem-based learning (PBL) activity and are divided into learning teams. The PBL case, described by Duncan (1999), is set in a distressed rural community college district in the Delta region of the mid-South. The topical emphasis of the PBL case is recast annually. Topics have included redesign of developmental programming, developing more effective K–12 linkages, reshaping workforce programming, building rural entrepreneurship systems, and so forth.

Each learning team presents a strategic plan for organizational and community change for review by a panel of college administrators and community researchers. Plans are evaluated based on creativity, knowledge of organizational realities, community change processes, practicality, and brevity. After completing the program, participants who choose to do so can earn three semester hours of graduate credit by participating in follow-up activities.

Strategies used to bring continuity to the MCCFP process include the annual Phil Hardin Leadership Symposium, a lecture by a nationally known community college leader. This event is held in conjunction with the Mississippi Association of Colleges' annual fall conference. Previous symposium speakers include George Vaughan, Steve Katsinas, Jeff Hockaday, Dale Parnell, Rosemary Gillett-Karam, Barbara Townsend, Mark Musick, Terry Whisnant, and Tony Kinkel.

As a follow-up to the symposium, a committee of fellows plans activities in conjunction with the Creating Futures Through Technology winter conference, a program developed by the Mississippi State Board for Community and Junior Colleges. In addition, all MCCFP fellows are invited to share an evening at the MCCFP summer leadership retreat. This event includes a reception, an out-of-state speaker, and a social activity. Many community college presidents from the mid-South region usually attend this retreat. To date, MCCFP has served 301 community college professionals in nine states. Since the program was initiated, four fellows have assumed presidencies and forty-three report career advancement.

Community College Leadership Program

In June 1998, university and community college presidents; community and economic developers; faculty from colleges of education, arts, sciences, business, and agriculture; philanthropic interests; national associations; and governing board members convened to discuss the leader formation needs of Mississippi's community colleges. Discussions were framed around strengthening the community and economic development role of rural community colleges (Katsinas and Krebs, 1998). One of the strongest recommendations emerging from the conference was that several graduate degree programs, designed to meet the needs of rural community colleges and their communities, should be developed.

In addition, the conference attendees recommended creating a partnership among Mississippi's community colleges and land-grant universities. Alcorn State University (ASU) and Mississippi State University (MSU) joined with community colleges in the region to ensure that MSP would be a continuing collaboration. Today a master of arts in workforce development leadership is jointly granted by ASU and MSU, and each institution provides a master of arts in teaching with a community college emphasis. Both programs prepare students to serve as community college teachers.

Following the 1998 conference, the MSP conducted a five-state survey to determine the need for further academic programming. The survey and accompanying research confirmed the need for a doctoral program focused on the community-building role of rural college leaders. Mississippi's Institutions of Higher Learning board approved a Ph.D. program in community college leadership in January 2000. Board policy required MSU to assume degree-granting authority for the Community College Leadership program.

Lovell and others (2003) point out that CCL course work does not emphasize the broader field of higher education, nor does it focus on pedagogy. Rather, the program explores the interdisciplinary components that affect community and economic development in rural areas. The curriculum includes courses in rural sociology, rural community and economic development, rural government administration, public program evaluation, regional economics, and applied regional economics. In addition, students are required to complete a set of research requirements and community college leadership courses that emphasize "community" as well as "college."

Most CCL courses are taught by full-time university faculty. Additional instructional support comes from active community college leaders, including the executive director of the state coordinating board, university faculty with experience in community college leadership, university-based community and economic development professionals, and retired community college presidents.

Recently Clark (2006) evaluated the CCL program and explored student and alumni perceptions. Since its inception in 2000, 177 students have enrolled in the CCL program. Over 80 percent of the students enrolled have

NEW DIRECTIONS FOR COMMUNITY COLLEGES • DOI: 10.1002/cc

participated in the MCCFP. Of these students, 21 have completed their doc-torates, including 5 African Americans. The "grow-your-own approach," which begins with institutional nomination to the MCCFP and is then car-ried forward through the CCL program, has resulted in individual career advancement within and beyond the nominating institution. This career lad-der is clearly reflected among Clark's respondents, as most serve as directors, coordinators, and instructors in rural community colleges. The courses per-ceived by students as the most valuable were those focusing on rural com-munity and economic development, rural government, and community college finance and budgeting.

Building Research Support Systems

Linking community college leader development and rural community eco-nomic development requires continuing research support. The MSP addresses this challenge through three strategies: funded research, doctoral dissertation support, and technical assistance to colleges. Congressionally approved awards from the Fund for the Improvement of Postsecondary Education have accelerated the MSP's capacity for research activities.

The MSP's research agenda was set during a 1998 convention of commu-nity college presidents and researchers. This committee's initial recom-mendations were reviewed by the MSP's advisory council, which includes community college practitioners, community and economic developers, pol-icymakers, university-based researchers in departments of education, econom-ics, rural sociology, and political science. This process ultimately resulted in several areas of defined research. A joint committee of ASU and MSU faculty and administrators evaluated these goals and awarded the research contracts.

The initial funded research project was a comprehensive public policy study titled "Invigorating Rural Economies: The Rural Development Mis-sion of Mississippi's Community Colleges" (Rubin and others, 2005). An executive summary of this project was presented in January 2005 at the MCCFP state conference. Another MSP-funded research project reviewed how community colleges in the rural South create and support community self-identity and self-efficacy, and in process is a national study of commu-nity college barriers, incentives, and best practices in community develop-ment. Finally, a recent study examining Native American students in rural community colleges received the 2006 distinguished research award of the Mississippi Counseling Association (Watson, 2006).

These projects emphasize advancing college leadership capacity to engage in community economic development processes. For example, Rubin and others (2005) established five strategic imperatives for improv-ing Mississippi's rural economy. One imperative calls for the promotion of a culture of entrepreneurship. Thus, the problem-based learning case used in the summer 2005 MCCFP fellowship retreat was "entrepreneurship as a community development strategy." As a result, Mississippi's community and junior colleges have joined with the U.S. Department of Agriculture's Office of Rural Development to create and fund the Mississippi Entrepreneurial Alliance.

Support for students developing research topics that address rural college issues is provided through a competitive program called the Rural Doctoral Research Initiative (RDRI). Significant financial assistance for research and dissemination activities has been extended to approximately twenty students. Although a majority of these awards have been made to CCL students at Mississippi State University, students from other universities in and beyond the mid-South have received awards.

In addition, the MSP disseminates doctoral dissertations that address a variety of topics of concern to rural college leaders. Topics have included rural student retention and persistence, resource development, workforce development, student housing, athletics, nontraditional student services, and merit pay for faculty. Several RDRI projects have significant human capital enhancement policy implications. For example, Pugh (2006) suggests several state governing board and legislative actions that can stabilize workforce development funding.

The MSP also provides technical assistance to rural colleges and communities. This assistance takes several forms. For example, the MSP is supporting a community college–led development of an innovative software product that will facilitate the creation of strategic plans and support information synthesis by allowing data to be gathered, imported, and aggregated, forming a repository of information. At the same time, a system of interactive data warehousing is being developed for community college use, including analysis of local tax information by community college districts. The MSP has also delivered direct technical assistance to regional community colleges in order to support management systems reviews, strategic planning reviews, and resource development.

Links to State and National Rural Policy Organizations

In order to address ever-changing sociopolitical economics, the MSP has worked to forge relationships with a number of local and regional organizations For example, because community colleges in economically fragile communities are dependent on several federal agencies, the MSP has created a relationship with the United States Department of Agriculture to ensure support for student housing at the two hundred or so small rural colleges that offer residence halls. (See Chapter Eight in this volume for additional information on rural community college housing.) Community colleges also have a keen interest in the U.S. Department of Health and Human Services' Office of Rural Health Policy, because they are principal providers of training for rural allied health care workers.

NEW DIRECTIONS FOR COMMUNITY COLLEGES • DOI: 10.1002/cc

As a learning community of community college professionals, the MSP is connected to state and national organizations, including the Mississippi Association of Community and Junior Colleges and the State Board for Community and Junior Colleges. As well, the American Association of Community Colleges brings a national focus to issues touching all two-year colleges and offers a variety of leader development services for those in rural areas. These connections are especially important because there is a resource differential between rural, suburban, and urban colleges (see Chapter Two in this volume). Thus, building connections with those who have rural advocacy interests is an ongoing challenge.

Rural community college leaders must have experience with policy research and analysis practices and policy advocacy in local, state, and federal jurisdictions. As already noted, the MSP is organizationally linked to the John C. Stennis Institute of Government, a rural development–focused research and policy analysis unit at Mississippi State University. Faculty and staff associated with the Stennis Institute provide instruction in community college leadership courses, support the fellowship program, and guide doctoral and funded research projects. This reinforces and enriches the rural contextualization of the MSP's leader formation activities.

A key partner in regionalization or the development of multijurisdictional perspectives is the Southern Rural Development Center (SRDC) located at Mississippi State University. Because scale or institutional size frequently impedes rural development and rural community colleges, it is critical that college leaders look beyond jurisdictional boundaries and consider broader economic communities. The SRDC supports the community-building work of the twenty-nine land-grant universities of the mid-South region and has served as regional coordinator for the Rural Community College Initiative (Southern Rural Development Center, 2005). SRDC leadership provides instructional and research support to the MSP and fosters land-grant university–community college links across regions.

The MSP has also partnered with the Rural Community College Alliance and the Rural Policy Research Institute, a national rural policy research and analysis organization, to develop the National Institute for Rural Community Colleges. The institute provides a platform for building regional networks of outstanding programs serving rural colleges and communities and has fostered the Rural College Alliance, a collaboration of rural institutions in the United States and Canada.

Conclusion

The MSP and its partners have learned that creation and maintenance of cross-disciplinary, multisector learning communities is, in many ways, as countercultural for university personnel as it is for community college staff. Today's innovation can easily become tomorrow's turf. Thus, relationships

NEW DIRECTIONS FOR COMMUNITY COLLEGES • DOI: 10.1002/cc

between community colleges and universities must be continually nourished through communication and resources. The mission of helping people build sustainable rural communities requires continuing and direct experience and attention.

Continuous evaluation of programs and services is vital. Currently the MCCFP curriculum is undergoing review by university faculty and practitioners. For example, the curriculum used for the 2006 MCCFP retreat underwent substantial revision. Based on evaluation of those changes it is likely that both the format and curriculum will be altered in future years. In the CCL program, the need for more effective support for student research activities is currently under review. Program participants, university faculty, and representatives of the practitioner community are engaged together in these processes.

Presidential commitment at both the community college and university levels is essential. Formal institutional commitments are important, but the personal engagement of CEOs is also vital. There will be leadership turnover, and program proponents should take the lead in fostering executive conversations. Finally, state governing or coordinating board leadership is equally vital, and must be fostered. The leadership development activities of the MidSouth Partnership for Rural Community Colleges remain works in progress. Just as leader formation is a lifelong journey, so it is with building and linking processes and programs that support leaders.

References

Amey, M. J. "Leadership as Learning: Conceptualizing the Process." *Community College Journal of Research and Practice,* 2005, 29(9–10), 689–704.

Barnett, L., and others. *Opportunities in Place: National Assessment of the Rural Community College Initiative.* Washington, D.C.: Community College Press, 2003.

Bragg, D. D. "Doing Their Best: Exemplary Graduate Leadership Programs." *Community College Journal,* Aug.-Sept. 2002, pp. 49–53.

Clark, M. M. "An Assessment of the Community College Leadership Program at Mississippi State University as Perceived by Former and Current Students." Unpublished doctoral dissertation, Mississippi State University, 2006.

Duncan, C. M. *Worlds Apart: Why Poverty Persists in Rural America.* New Haven, Conn.: Yale University Press, 1999.

Katsinas, S., and Krebs, W. P. "The Proposed MidSouth Partnership for Rural Community Colleges: A Cooperative Effort of Mississippi State University and Alcorn State University." Summary of the MidSouth Partnership for Community Colleges Fellowship Program conference proceedings, Louisville, Miss., June 1998.

Lovell, N., and others. "The Road Less Traveled: Atypical Doctoral Preparation of Leaders in Rural Community Colleges." *Community College Journal of Research and Practice,* 2003, 27(1), 1–14.

Pugh, J. "An Exploration of Advantages Associated with Stable Funding for State Supported Workforce Education as an Impetus for Change in Mississippi's Funding of Workforce Education." Unpublished doctoral dissertation, Mississippi State University, 2006.

Rubin, S., and Autry, G. "Rural Community Colleges: Catalysts for Economic Renewal." ECS Policy Paper. Denver: Education Commission of the States, 1998.

Rubin, S., and others. "Invigorating Rural Economies: The Rural Development Mission of Mississippi's Community Colleges." Special Report of the MidSouth Partnership for Rural Community Colleges No. PSR 05–2. Meridian, Miss.: MidSouth Partnership for Rural Community Colleges, 2005.

Shults, C. *The Critical Impact of Impending Retirements on Community College Leadership.* Leadership Series Research Brief No. 1. Washington, D.C.: American Association of Community Colleges, 2001.

Southern Rural Development Center. "RCCI Year Three Report." Meridian, Miss.: Southern Rural Development Center, 2005. http://srdc.msstate.edu/rcci/reports/05report.pdf. Accessed Nov. 20, 2006.

Vaughn, G. B., and Weisman, I. M. *The Community College Presidency at the Millennium.* Washington, D.C.: Community College Press, 1998.

Watson, J. C. "The Retention of Native American Students at Mississippi Public Community Colleges: Examining the Influence of Racial Identity on College Adjustment." Meridian, Miss.: MidSouth Partnership for Rural Community Colleges, 2006.

Molly M. Clark is a graduate of the Community College Leadership doctoral program at Mississippi State University and lead online instructor for communication at Itawamba Community College, Mississippi.

Ed Davis is coordinator of community college programs at Mississippi State University.

*Much is being written about a potential shortage of quali-
fied community college faculty. Rural community colleges
may be at the greatest disadvantage in attracting and
retaining new faculty because they cannot offer the financial, cultural, and social advantages that more urban
institutions can. This chapter describes the factors rural
community college leaders must consider when recruiting
and hiring new professors.*

Recruiting and Retaining Rural Community College Faculty

John P. Murray

Many educators believe that because of unprecedented faculty attrition (Berry, Hammons, and Denny, 2001), rural community colleges will have difficulty recruiting and retaining qualified faculty (Leist, 2005). Nonetheless, there is a paucity of literature that specifically addresses faculty job satisfaction at community colleges, much less at rural community colleges. This chapter begins by describing the challenges presented by rural settings to those who might wish to teach at a rural community college and offers suggestions for recruiting and retaining faculty in a rural setting.

Challenges of the Rural Environment

Faculty members face a number of challenges when they accept a position at a rural community college. Prospective community college faculty members need to understand that individuals living in rural areas suffer from a number of social and economic ills. Rural areas often have high levels of illiteracy, low levels of educational attainment, high unemployment, and extreme poverty. Although not all rural communities are impoverished, many are. "Of the almost four hundred counties with poverty rates of 20 percent or greater in every decade since 1959, 95 percent are rural" (Mosley and Miller, 2004, p. 2).

The poverty of rural areas is exacerbated by the loss of industry and the consequent loss of employment opportunities. America's traditional rural

job base is rapidly disappearing. Agricultural and extractive industries, such as mining, fishing, and lumbering, are declining, and those that remain are frequently low-paying and subject to the whims of global and national economic downswings, causing frequent shutdowns and layoffs (Mosley and Miller, 2004). The manufacturing base of rural America has traditionally been low-paying and labor-intensive. However, many of these industries have automated and now require a highly skilled labor force. Unfortunately, because educational attainment in rural America is low, many of these industries have relocated to urban areas, seeking a better-educated workforce. Others have outsourced their jobs overseas in search of cheaper labor. The steady attrition of employment opportunities leaves rural communities "with relatively unskilled workforces, and without the necessary infrastructure to rebuild" (McNutt, 1994, p. 196).

The steady erosion of unskilled jobs negatively affects the educational environment of rural communities, and thus creates greater poverty. Many young people become discouraged over the lack of opportunities in their community and drop out of school. Those who graduate from high school or college often leave home in search of better jobs. Indeed, far fewer rural citizens hold college degrees than their metropolitan counterparts. "As of 2001, more than 26 percent of metropolitan residents possessed at least a college degree, compared to only 15 percent of those in nonmetropolitan areas" (Mosley and Miller, 2004, p. 5).

Rural community colleges represent hope for a better future for rural citizens. In *Worlds Apart: Why Poverty Persists in Rural America,* Duncan (1999) wrote: "A good education is the key that unlocks and expands the cultural toolkits of the have-nots, and thus gives them the potential to bring about lasting social change in their persistently poor communities" (p. 208). Although education may be seen as a way to reduce poverty, some researchers (Mosley and Miller, 2004) have found that education has less of an effect on rural Americans than on metropolitan residents. This may be partially explained by the relocation of educated youths; although a college education may be seen as a ticket out of poverty, it is also too often a ticket out of the rural community (McNutt, 1994). This exportation of many individuals who could assist in the revitalization of rural communities only intensifies the poverty and leaves behind the elderly, the unskilled, and the undereducated. An overlooked outcome of this outmigration of educated citizens is the effect on the tax base. The loss of educated individuals places the tax burden on those least able to pay additional taxes to support a community college or any educational institution.

The impoverished tax base and lower levels of educational attainment in rural communities present several challenges for those developing curricula at rural community colleges. When it comes to funding, rural community colleges suffer a double bind. States expect the local community to contribute to the funding of the local community college. They also expect the individuals who will benefit from the education to pay their fair share through tuition and fees. However, because many rural communities are poverty-stricken and have a low tax base, they are hard-pressed to support a community college, and the residents have little disposable income to spend on tuition (Higgins and Katsinas, 1999; McNutt, 1994). This means that there is not much money for high-cost curricula, adjunct or full-time faculty salaries, or faculty development. Often rural community colleges cannot afford to provide high-cost technical programs. Furthermore, even if they have the resources, they may be unable to find qualified faculty who will relocate for the salary they can pay. This often forces rural community colleges to offer less costly transfer curricular. Students who transfer are less likely to return to the rural community, which further drains the educated individuals from rural communities.

Recruiting Faculty

Although many believe that a severe shortage of faculty is not yet upon us, several commentators have noted that in highly specialized disciplines the crisis is already here (Burnett, 2004; Evelyn, 2001; Leist, 2005). "Already, colleges have seen shortages in qualified faculty in areas like math, science, nursing, technology, special education, and English as a Second Language" (Burnett, 2004, p. 7). Moreover, for rural community colleges the state of affairs is a bit more complicated than just recruiting faculty to teach highly specialized courses. Increasingly, it is also difficult to find faculty in less specialized areas, including some that once produced an abundance of applicants. An administrator at one rural community college complained that "while fifteen years ago, an English faculty opening would bring in about 150 applicants, today the number is closer to 30 applicants. And if there are 10 of those who are qualified, it's unusual" (Burnett, 2004, p. 8). Because there are usually few local citizens who are qualified to teach at a community college, college leaders often must try to convince individuals to move to their communities. Despite what may be a bucolic setting, the lack of cultural, social, shopping, and recreational amenities in rural areas makes for a tough sell in recruiting new faculty (Leist, 2005). Daniel P. Doherty, the dean of instruction at Western Nebraska Community College, put it this way: "We have a lot of trouble just getting them in the door, just to see the campuses. . . . [S]omeone has to know this country and want to come here" (Burnett, 2004, p. 7).

Rural community colleges are also hard-pressed to recruit a racially and ethnically diverse faculty. It is often very hard to recruit minorities to move to rural communities. Also problematic is the recruitment of an intellectually diverse faculty. For rural community colleges it is often easiest to recruit from nearby universities, which can lead to an intellectually insular faculty.

NEW DIRECTIONS FOR COMMUNITY COLLEGES • DOI: 10.1002/cc

Retaining Faculty

Even when faculty are successfully recruited to a rural community college, it can be difficult to retain them. Many community colleges are experiencing an unprecedented turnover in early and midcareer faculty: "Many of the faculty who leave early go back to earn their doctorates. . . . Others go to work at larger community colleges" (Burnett, 2004, p. 8). This is a serious problem for rural community colleges, given the difficulty they face recruiting full-time faculty.

Organizational theorists, including those who study higher education, stress that the way in which an employee is socialized into a profession is often critical to the willingness of novice employees to remain with the institution and the career (Aryee, Chay, and Chew, 1994). Moreover, the literature suggests that new faculty members are much more likely to be successfully socialized into the profession when they have realistic expectations of what it will entail (Feldman, 1981; Gaff and Lambert, 1996). This also seems to be the case at rural community colleges (Murray, 2005; Murray and Cunningham, 2004).

Some organizational theorists note that met expectations theory best explains career commitment, voluntary job turnover, and job satisfaction (Aryee, Chay, and Chew, 1994; Aryee and Tan, 1992). Individuals whose expectations of the job are more closely aligned with the reality of the job are more likely to experience job satisfaction, and therefore, more likely to find a career fit. Organizational researchers have concluded that person-environment fit best accounts for job satisfaction (Bertz and Judge, 1994). Individuals whose expectations are met tend to have higher job satisfaction, and those with higher job satisfaction are judged by superiors as being better performers, are more committed to the organization, and have longer tenures.

What should new rural community college faculty members expect? As the saying goes, there is good news and bad news. The bad news is not always unique to rural colleges. All community colleges share some features that can cause a new faculty member discomfort if he or she is unaware of them. Although new faculty members are aware that community colleges are open admissions institutions, the uninitiated are often shocked when they realize the range of student abilities they will face in the classroom. Sax, Astin, Korn, and Gilmartin (1999) found that 80 percent of community college faculty members believe that their students are less academically prepared than they should be for the rigors of college-level work.

Another potential shock for those not familiar with the community college environment is the heavy workload. At most community colleges, faculty teach five to six courses an academic term and spend between fifteen and twenty-eight hours a week in instructional settings. In addition, they are often expected to advise students, serve on committees, and do community service. Yet another surprise for the unaware is the repetitive nature of the work. Community college faculty usually teach the same three or four introductory courses year after year, with little opportunity to teach advanced courses in their discipline.

The innocent often fail to realize that they will have little time to pursue more specialized academic interests, and this can lead to a kind of intellectual estrangement from the discipline. There is little or no time to pursue research or even to read professional journals. For faculty at rural community colleges, this sense of professional isolation is further exacerbated by the fact that an instructor may be the sole faculty teaching in a discipline. In addition to being cut off from colleagues who share their academic interests, these one-person "departments" increase these faculty members' workload. The instructor must carry the entire burden of advising majors, developing and keeping the curriculum up to date, coordinating articulation agreements or job placement programs, and recruiting new students.

Rural community colleges face at least one more unique concern when trying to recruit and retain faculty: location. The faculty members who express the most satisfaction with teaching at a rural community college are those who are comfortable living and working in a rural community. It can be very difficult to recruit individuals to a rural area for the many quality-of-life reasons discussed earlier in this chapter. Moreover, once faculty are recruited, it can be difficult to retain those who have no previous experience living in a rural area. This can be a serious concern for minorities when there are few other minorities in the community. Moreover, for dual-career couples, there is often little opportunity for employment for the spouse.

If we are to help prospective rural faculty members develop realistic expectations that might lead them to stay, we should also explain the joys rural community college faculty find in their work. Study after study has found that the majority of community college faculty members find teaching to be a satisfying career; overwhelmingly, faculty report that their greatest satisfaction comes from teaching. Ironically, they also often tell researchers that it is the teaching of the unprepared or underachieving student that is most satisfying (Wolfe and Strange, 2003).

Suggestions for Recruiting and Retaining Faculty

Given what has been said about the rural environment, how should community colleges go about recruiting and retaining faculty? The following suggestions are drawn from my own previous research as well as my experience at a rural community college.

Recruitment. The following may be helpful in recruiting faculty to rural community colleges.

Look Carefully in Your Own Backyard. Community college leaders looking for new faculty might start by involving current faculty in the recruitment process. One study (Murray and Cunningham, 2004) found that many new faculty said they had been recruited by other faculty. A number of participants also mentioned that they had been adjuncts before becoming full-time.

Think Family. Often dual-career couples settle in metropolitan areas because there are employment opportunities for both individuals. Many times an individual can be recruited if there is also a possibility of employment for a trailing spouse. The position can be a staff position, or if the spouse is qualified, a faculty position. Employing two members of a household also increases the likelihood of retaining both.

Look Far and Wide. Many individuals like the idea of living in rural settings. Contact universities with graduate programs (especially those with large master's programs) and discuss the advantages of your community. These may be access to national or state parks, lakes, or historic sites; the low cost of living; good school systems; and so forth. Offer to sponsor a weekend visit to the community for interested candidates. This is also a good time to make prospective candidates aware of opportunities for their significant others.

Take a Risk. Creative rural community colleges leaders might consider creating a teaching fellows program. Such a program would recruit recent graduates or students finishing their dissertations and provide them with a mentor, a title, and a promise of gaining experience. It would also give the college an opportunity to convince the best graduates to stay at the college.

Grow Your Own. Keep track of community college students who have transferred to four-year colleges. Some of them will go on to obtain an advanced degree and may welcome the opportunity to return and teach in the community they grew up in.

Retention. Once a faculty member is recruited, the next challenge is to retain that individual. If rural community colleges wish to retain faculty, they will need to be innovative. For so long, community college leaders have not had to concern themselves with the needs of the faculty. Until recently, there has been a plentiful supply of candidates and a shortage of openings. In a tight job market, retention becomes a minor issue because those with jobs are much less likely to have opportunities to leave. However, with the potential of a large turnover at both four-year colleges and community colleges, administrators will find it necessary to be more concerned with meeting the needs of faculty.

Individuals tend to leave positions for a variety of reasons; some we can control and some we cannot. Among the main reasons for leaving a position are burnout, the feeling that the compensation is inadequate, the lack of job security, and the perception that the quality of life is poor. Although institutional leaders cannot always control these factors, they can ameliorate them to some extent.

The most difficult of these factors for administrators to deal with are job security and compensation issues. Leaders can work hard to devise a fair compensation package. For many prospective employees the fringe benefits package is often extremely important. Employers who offer a generous package will have an advantage.

Although not all the factors contributing to burnout can be addressed by administrators, some common causes can be addressed. Burnout is often caused by the repetitious nature of teaching the same courses year after year. Consider providing faculty with avenues for professional growth such as funds for travel to professional conferences, the latest technology, seed money for small research projects, assistance in preparing manuscripts, and release time to develop new curricula. Also consider moving faculty out of the classroom for periods of time by assigning them to special projects or having them temporarily take an administrative role when an employee suddenly leaves or takes an extended leave of absence.

For many faculty and staff, balancing work and family obligations is a great stressor (Luce and Murray, 1998). Young families have to balance child rearing, and older families are often faced with helping aging parents. Community colleges can help reduce the stress by providing flexible work hours, assistance with day care, and flexible family leave plans.

Among the reasons for leaving that community college leaders can control is the perception that one's contribution to the college is not being appreciated. Recognition of excellence need not be costly. When faculty are recognized for their accomplishments, they develop professional pride, and professional pride can be a powerful motivator. Faculty recognized for excellence might be given a teaching award with or without a modest stipend, a title such as faculty associate or teaching mentor, a plaque, a framed certificate, a gift certificate from a bookstore or restaurant, a close-by parking space, or lunch with the president.

Conclusion

Rural community colleges can do a better job of recruiting and retaining faculty if they take the time and effort to develop orientation programs that introduce prospective faculty to the realities of teaching and living in a rural community college. Those realities include a heavy workload, life in a rural community, and teaching a socially and economically diverse student body that may be underprepared for college-level work. When researchers examine the reasons for staying or leaving a college, several things stand out. Those wishing to stay are also those who find it satisfying to work with a diverse student body. They want to teach individuals, not just a subject matter. They believe that what they are doing is important and valued by others. In other words, faculty who have realistic expectations about their jobs will find it satisfying when those expectations are met. Recruiting and retaining good employees do not just happen. In a tight market, wise community college leaders need to carefully plan for and work at maintaining an excellent faculty.

References

Aryee, S., Chay, Y. W., and Chew, J. "An Investigation of the Predictors and Outcomes of Career Commitment in Three Career Stages." *Journal of Vocational Behavior*, 1994, *44*, 1–16.

Aryee, S., and Tan, K. "Antecedents and Outcomes of Career Commitment." *Journal of Vocational Behavior*, 1992, *40*, 288–305.

Berry, L. H., Hammons, J. O., and Denny, G. S. "Faculty Retirement Turnover in Community Colleges: A Real or Imagined Problem?" *Community College Journal of Research and Practice*, 2001, *25*, 123–136.

Bertz, R. D., and Judge, T. A. "Person-Organization Fit and the Theory of Work Adjustment: Implications for Satisfaction, Tenure, and Career Success." *Journal of Vocational Behavior*, 1994, *44*, 32–52.

Burnett, S. "Using Our Imagination." *Community College Week*, 2004, *17*(4), 6–8.

Duncan, C. (1999). *Worlds Apart: Why Poverty Persists in Rural America.* New Haven, Conn.: Yale University Press, 1999.

Evelyn, J. "The Hiring Boom at Two-Year Colleges." *Chronicle of Higher Education*, 2001, *47*(40), A8–A9.

Feldman, D. C. "The Multiple Socialization of Organization Members." *Academy of Management Review*, 1981, *6*, 301–318.

Gaff, J. G., and Lambert, L. M. "Socializing Future Faculty to the Values of Undergraduate Education." *Change*, 1996, *4*, 39–45.

Higgins, S. C., and Katsinas, S. G. "The Relationship Between Environmental Conditions and Transfer Rates of Selected Rural Community Colleges: A Pilot Study." *Community College Review*, 1999, *2*(27), 1–25.

Leist, J. E. "Exemplary Rural Community College Presidents: A Case Study of How Well Their Professional Qualities Mirror Job Advertisements." Unpublished doctoral dissertation, Texas Tech University, 2005.

Luce, J., and Murray, J. P. "New Faculty's Perceptions of Academic Work Life." *Journal of Staff, Program, & Organizational Development*, 1998, *15*(3), 103–110.

McNutt, A. S. "Rural Community Colleges: Meeting the Challenges of the 1990s." In G. A. Baker III, J. Dudziak, and P. Tyler (eds.), *A Handbook on the Community College in America: Its History, Mission, and Management.* Westport, Conn.: Greenwood, 1994.

Mosley, J. M., and Miller, K. K. *What the Research Says About Spatial Variations in Factors Affecting Poverty.* Research Brief 2004–1. Corvallis: Oregon State University, Rural Poverty Research Center, 2004.

Murray, J. P. "Meeting the Needs of New Faculty at Rural Community Colleges." *Community College Journal of Research and Practice*, 2005, *29*(3), 215–232.

Murray, J. P., and Cunningham, S. "New Community College Faculty Members and Job Satisfaction." *Community College Review*, 2004, *32*(2), 19–32.

Sax, L. J., Astin, A. W., Korn, W. S., and Gilmartin, S. K. *The American College Teacher: National Norms for the 1998–1999 HERI Faculty Survey.* Los Angeles: University of California, Higher Education Research Institute, 1999.

Wolfe, J. R., and Strange, C. C. "Academic Life at the Franchise: Faculty Culture in a Rural Two-Year Branch Campus." *Review of Higher Education*, 2003, *26*(3), 343–362.

JOHN P. MURRAY *is professor of higher education at Texas Tech University and program director for the higher education administration program.*

NEW DIRECTIONS FOR COMMUNITY COLLEGES • DOI: 10.1002/cc

7

This chapter describes results from a national study of community college faculty development programs. Findings highlight how the challenges faced by rural colleges differ from those at urban institutions, which often have dedicated faculty development centers.

Faculty Development in Rural Community Colleges

Pamela L. Eddy

Faculty choose to teach in rural areas for a variety of reasons. As Vander-Staay (2005) notes, rural institutions have the privileges of bucolic and beautiful natural settings, faculty have shorter commutes, and the institutions tend to value teaching. However, he also points out that teaching in a rural area often means that one has sole responsibility for the curriculum, few if any peers in the same discipline, and a lower salary than at an urban community college.

Many of the challenges that faculty face at rural community colleges are similar to those faculty face across the educational continuum—namely, navigating and balancing multiple demands because of shifts in institutional and student needs, a push to implement student-centered learning, increased community outreach, and the use of technology in teaching. However, rural faculty have fewer resources than instructors at urban and suburban community colleges, face different student needs, and must wear many hats. For example, rural faculty often must provide additional help to students, whereas larger or more urban institutions may have tutoring centers available. As well, rural community college faculty may have to manage science and technology labs without the support of a paid lab director or provide regional expertise to businesses and communities. For some faculty, the rural context can mean isolation, fewer cultural activities, and the need to travel for shopping and entertainment (Murray, 2005; Wolfe and Strange, 2003).

NEW DIRECTIONS FOR COMMUNITY COLLEGES, no. 137, Spring 2007 © 2007 Wiley Periodicals, Inc.
Published online in Wiley InterScience (www.interscience.wiley.com) • DOI: 10.1002/cc.271

Despite the challenges facing rural community college faculty, benefits are equally prevalent. For some faculty, the draw is the beauty of the rural region. Simple living, safe communities, and outdoor recreation provide a draw and attraction to these areas. For others, the ability to have a significant impact on the direction of a department and program, to directly see the outcomes of learning for students, and to be intimately tied to making improvements to the regional economy are the benefits of teaching in a rural college.

To aid and support rural community college faculty, professional development programs and activities are essential. In all community colleges, both urban and rural, faculty development has a relatively short history as an institutionally supported initiative. In a review of the history of faculty development, Sorcinelli, Austin, Eddy, and Beach (2006) describe four previous ages of faculty development—the age of the scholar, the age of the teacher, the age of the developer, and the age of the learner. They propose we are in a new age—the age of the network—which requires increased collaboration and connections for both student and faculty learning.

Sorcinelli, Austin, Eddy, and Beach's (2006) hypothesis has many implications for faculty development in rural community colleges. However, most of the research conducted on faculty development in institutions of higher education focuses on four-year colleges (Centra, 1976; Erickson, 1986). Prior to the study described in this chapter, only one national survey was conducted on faculty development in public two-year colleges (Murray, 2001). The primary purpose of Murray's study was to enumerate the types of programs and activities in community college faculty development programs and centers. He found that faculty development at community colleges encompassed little more than random activities, and that faculty development programming at two-year colleges lacked intentionality. This conclusion mirrors Cohen and Brawer's (2003) finding that community colleges have historically chosen not to create centralized units for professional development, instead hiring appropriately trained staff or providing inservice training when necessary.

This chapter describes research conducted to create a portrait of faculty development at community colleges and asks if there are significant differences in community college faculty development needs based on college location. After briefly describing the methodology used to conduct the study, this chapter reviews the challenges identified by faculty developers, provides a portrait of faculty development at community colleges, and identifies the goals, current practices, and new directions guiding rural faculty development efforts. The chapter concludes with implications for faculty development in rural areas.

Methodology

Data informing this research were collected via a survey sent to a stratified random sample of community college academic vice presidents and the designated leaders of faculty development programs. The mailing list for vice presidents was obtained from the American Association of Community Colleges. Once the sample of vice presidents was compiled, names of individual faculty development directors at each institution were culled from the National Council for Staff, Program, and Organizational Development's online member registry. If a name was not available, the survey was addressed to the faculty development director at the institution. Because that title is not as common in rural community colleges, the persons leading faculty development efforts on campus are referred to as *leaders of development efforts* for the remainder of this chapter. A total of 497 institutions was selected, and both the academic vice president and the faculty development director at each college received a survey. The response rate for vice presidents was 43 percent; it was 36 percent for leaders of professional development. The overall survey response rate was 39 percent, possibly because we did not have names for all those leading development efforts.

The survey consisted of four-point scaled sections, identification of priority rankings, and open-ended questions that provided an opportunity for respondents to more fully explicate their conceptions of the direction of faculty development. Respondents were asked about the structure of faculty development programs in their colleges, the goals guiding faculty development programming, the top three priorities guiding programming decisions, and the most pressing current issues and new directions in faculty development efforts. Demographic data were also collected about the size of the college, its location (rural, suburban, urban), titles of the respondents, including identification of primary title, years of service as a professional developer, and other individual characteristics. Survey responses were entered into SPSS for analysis. Descriptive statistical analysis is reported here to show preliminary information about the context in which rural community college faculty development efforts occur, and to provide a portrait of important current and new directions of practice. This chapter reports responses from both vice presidents and leaders of faculty development.

Challenges for Rural Faculty

Considering that 60 percent of all community colleges are located in rural areas, it is not surprising that 46.8 percent of survey respondents stated that they worked in a rural location. Another 28.2 percent worked in a suburban college, 16.7 percent worked in urban locales, and another 8.3 percent worked in urban areas with suburban branch campuses. The findings reported in this chapter compare survey responses from vice presidents and faculty development directors at rural community colleges to those from all other types of institutions (for the purposes of this chapter, this aggregated category will be called "urban").

New Directions for Community Colleges • DOI: 10.1002/cc

Survey respondents were asked to identify the top three challenges community college faculty face. The top challenges mentioned by both urban and rural community college faculty development leaders were the same, but the levels of intensity differed. The top two challenges identified were *assessment of student learning* and *working with underprepared students.* For both these challenges, urban leaders of faculty development efforts rated these program areas as more important than those leading efforts in rural areas. Almost half of the urban developers (47 percent) rated assessment of student learning as the biggest challenge, whereas only 38 percent of rural faculty developers rated assessment as a faculty challenge. Likewise, more urban respondents rated working with underprepared students higher (42 percent) than rural developers (33 percent). Thus, although these issues were identified as critical to faculty in both urban and rural areas, they were thought to be more important to leaders of development efforts in urban areas. Perhaps this is because assessment programs are easier to implement on a smaller scale and therefore present less of a challenge for smaller rural colleges. Implementing assessment in larger urban districts, which involves more degree options and course work, may result in more complex planning for assessment. Moreover, larger student populations in urban community colleges translate to a wider variety of student abilities—particularly those students requiring remediation.

When looking at other faculty challenges, both rural and urban community college faculty developers identified the challenges of *integrating technology into traditional classroom teaching* and *balancing faculty roles.* These areas are considered to be secondary challenges, because only one-quarter of leaders of development identified them. In these instances, there was more agreement between those leading efforts in rural and urban areas. In addition to these secondary challenges, rural faculty also identified a few other challenges, including *program assessment* (20 percent), *student-centered learning* (19 percent), *teaching online* (17 percent), and *training part-time and adjunct faculty* (17 percent). With fewer resources, rural community colleges need to be selective in the types of programming offered—hence the challenge of assessing programs to determine those most viable. The focus on student-centered learning becomes important in rural areas because faculty teach smaller classes and can adapt to meet student needs. One means for rural colleges to increase resources is extending their offerings online. To do so, however, requires faculty trained for online teaching. Finally, although rural colleges employ fewer part-time faculty, these faculty still require training to be most effective. The lack of a specific infrastructure in rural locales for training adjunct faculty presents a challenge, because the numbers requiring the training are smaller than in urban areas that may have dedicated staff for these training purposes. Clearly, rural community college developers saw a broader array of challenges facing their faculty than did their urban counterparts. The fact that there are fewer faculty in rural areas means that

NEW DIRECTIONS FOR COMMUNITY COLLEGES • DOI: 10.1002/cc

these faculty have responsibility for more of the duties required to support classroom learning. The larger number of urban faculty mean that responsibilities can be shared among a greater faculty base.

Also notable were the different levels of importance reported by rural and urban developers. Even though these challenges were not identified with high frequency, there were marked differences based on college location. Shifting student demographics (rural 4 percent, urban 10 percent) and dealing with multicultural differences (rural 4 percent, urban 9 percent) were challenges noted more often in urban areas. Institutional issues of departmental leadership (rural 12 percent, urban 9 percent) and preparing future faculty (rural 9 percent, urban 5 percent) were more often noted by rural respondents.

More agreement was found in responses from urban developers as represented by larger percentages of respondents indicating an item as one of the top three challenges facing faculty and the institution. Rural colleges focused more on broader issues and were also concerned with departmental leadership and training future faculty, because they make greater use of full-time faculty and the pool from which departmental leaders may be drawn is smaller. Urban colleges noted more challenges when it came to dealing with multicultural issues and shifting student demographics. Rural areas tend to be more homogenous in their populations, and given their isolated locations, have not seen the influx of the variety of students of color more likely in urban regions.

Portrait of Faculty Development

Women are less likely to lead faculty development in rural community colleges than they are in urban campuses (47 and 65 percent, respectively). In rural locations, senior-level administrators (60 percent) or midlevel administrators (11 percent) were most likely to have filled out the survey, with named directors of faculty development completing another 12 percent of responses. Even though some faculty development efforts were led by a person with the title of faculty development director, these individuals most often had another title as well, either administrator or faculty member. In urban campuses, however, 18 percent of respondents were faculty development directors, 44 percent were senior administrators, and 10 percent were midlevel administrators. Furthermore, only 8 percent of urban respondents indicated that they were faculty members, whereas faculty made up 17 percent of the respondents from rural colleges.

Both rural and urban leaders of faculty development efforts were overseen by administrators. However, administrators led faculty development efforts in rural areas more often than in urban areas (71 percent compared to 54 percent). It can be hypothesized that administrators leading efforts in urban areas are assigning actual programming responsibilities to others, whereas administrators in rural areas are directly leading programming efforts. In addition, more faculty members led efforts in rural areas

NEW DIRECTIONS FOR COMMUNITY COLLEGES • DOI: 10.1002/cc

(17 percent) than in urban areas (8 percent). Greater administrative leadership in faculty development programming in rural community colleges means that a more global perspective can be achieved, and faculty development programming can focus on issues that will help meet institutional goals as well as individual faculty goals. Although the desires of the institution and faculty may overlap, administrators frequently prefer improvement of institutional outcomes. The high level of individual faculty involvement in leading development efforts at rural community colleges indicates that decisions about programming also have a faculty voice. Working in a smaller institution, however, means that faculty may also see the direct impact of their work on larger institutional goals, whereas urban faculty leading development efforts may focus more on the issues facing faculty in the classroom. The larger infrastructure of urban community colleges allows for a director to oversee the function of faculty development.

A key difference in the portrait of rural community colleges compared to urban colleges emerges in how respondents describe their faculty development structure. In rural areas, most faculty development efforts are led either by a committee (35 percent) or an individual faculty member (33 percent). Similarly, in urban areas 33 percent of faculty development efforts are led by committee and 19 percent are led by individual faculty members. However, differences emerge in the degree of centralization of faculty development efforts. Urban community colleges have more centralized development (17 percent report use of a center, and 10 percent use a central clearinghouse). However, on rural campuses only 10 percent of respondents reported the existence of a faculty development center and 9 percent stated that they use a development clearinghouse. Finally, although both urban and rural community colleges use blended programming—in other words, a combination of committees, individual faculty leaders, clearinghouses, or dedicated faculty development centers—urban colleges reported more blended programming (15 percent) than rural campuses (9 percent). The use of various programming approaches in urban colleges correlates to more focused efforts on faculty development at these campuses.

Programming decisions are affected by the structures in place for faculty development oversight. The formal structure for development efforts at rural colleges was most often at a simpler level—namely, provided by an individual or a committee of faculty. The fact that faculty also have classroom responsibilities means that less programming might be available at rural institutions in comparison to urban community colleges. Urban colleges may also have the support of programming offered by other units in the college, such as a technology department or human resources. The fact that almost 30 percent of urban colleges had a dedicated faculty development center or clearinghouse for programming efforts means that dedicated resources were more available for faculty development on urban campuses.

Development Program Goals

Given a list of nine goals frequently used to guide faculty development programming, survey respondents were asked to rate each goal on the degree to which it helped guide their campus's programming efforts. Respondents were also asked to indicate the top three goals that were primary to their planning. Although urban and rural college respondents both listed the same three primary goals, there were a few differences between the two types of institutions. For example, a majority of urban and rural respondents (67.8 and 64.5 percent, respectively) indicated that the goal of *creating and sustaining a culture of excellence in teaching* was of utmost importance. As well, 59 percent of rural respondents and 57.3 percent of those from urban areas indicated that *responding to individual faculty members' goals for development* was a primary goal. However, only 47.4 percent of rural respondents indicated that *advancing new initiatives in teaching and learning* was a primary goal, compared to 60.9 percent of urban respondents. Even though half of the rural developers were interested in bringing new classroom strategies to their faculty, urban planners showed more agreement on this program goal. All of the primary goals for both rural and urban faculty developers focused on classroom teaching, learning issues, and the needs of individual faculty. A clear dedication to teaching support is behind programming decisions. Less attention to new initiatives on rural campuses highlights a need to focus first on meeting the demands already evident without stretching resources too thin. Given the broader array of faculty challenges outlined by rural developers, it is clear that development support is required to aid faculty in fulfilling their classroom functions.

Rural and urban respondents differed even more on the importance of secondary goals—those items not listed as the top three priorities. For example, 40 percent of faculty development leaders in rural colleges identified *responding to critical needs of the institution,* 23 percent identified *supporting departmental goals and needs,* and 21 percent identified *acting as a change agent* as important, but not primary, goals. Rural faculty developers agreed that institutional issues guide programming efforts to a larger extent than for their urban counterparts. For urban developers, in contrast, *responding to critical needs of the institution* was of secondary importance (28 percent), although roughly the same percentage of urban as rural developers (24 and 21 percent, respectively) indicated that *acting as a change agent* was important. Rural developers were twice as likely (23 percent) as urban leaders (12 percent) to indicate that their programming efforts also intended to support departmental goals and planning. Leaders of development efforts in urban areas more often stated a goal of providing training for part-time and adjunct faculty (19 percent) than those in urban areas (13 percent). Clearly, institutional improvement issues are closely tied to development programming at rural community colleges.

NEW DIRECTIONS FOR COMMUNITY COLLEGES • DOI: 10.1002/cc

Factors Influencing Faculty Development Programs

Individuals responsible for faculty development programming receive input from and are influenced by a variety of sources. Respondents rated these sources on a scale of one to four, with four indicating greatest influence. Urban and rural faculty developers rated these influences similarly. For example, both types of faculty rated college teaching and learning literature highly, although urban respondents rated this influence slightly higher (mean = 3.56) than rural respondents (3.41). As well, both gave literature on community colleges (3.32 and 3.36, respectively) and literature on faculty development (3.30 and 3.20) similar ratings of importance. Both urban and rural respondents listed the American Association of Community Colleges as influential in designing faculty development programming (mean ratings were 2.92 and 2.94, respectively). Finally, urban and rural respondents identified similar influences on their thinking about their approach to faculty development on campus. Both urban and rural respondents indicated that they were influenced by *a commitment to student learning* (3.88 and 3.81, respectively) and *a commitment to promoting good teaching* (3.83 and 3.76, respectively). Institutional leadership also influences faculty development programming at urban and rural community colleges (3.22 and 3.29, respectively), as does campus culture (3.28 and 3.26). Finally, both types of respondents indicated that time spent as a faculty member helped them make decisions about program planning (3.14 and 3.04, respectively).

Essentially, all planners of development efforts, regardless of rural or urban locale, are influenced by the same literature base and individual goals. The literature on teaching and learning and faculty development helps shape the ways that leaders of faculty development create programming on their campuses. However, both urban and rural faculty development leaders see the American Association of Community Colleges (AACC) as only moderately influential in how they then plan for training on their campuses. The larger leadership development focus of the AACC may be a reason for this, but AACC leaders could enhance their impact on community college campuses by focusing on faculty development at the grassroots level with direct ties to the classroom. The influences on leaders of faculty development have a direct impact on the focus of current practices and new directions in faculty training.

Current Practices and New Directions for Rural Faculty Development

Community college faculty developers and administrators were asked to list the faculty development practices they currently offer, and rate a list of twenty common practices on a scale from one to four by level of importance. Rural community college developers offered the following activities to a moderate extent: *integrating technology into traditional teaching and learning activities* (mean = 3.43), *teaching online* (3.30), and *assessment of student*

NEW DIRECTIONS FOR COMMUNITY COLLEGES • DOI: 10.1002/cc

learning (3.07). Urban campuses offer the following programming to a moderate or great extent: *integrating technology into classrooms* (3.57), *teaching online* (3.38), and *implementing student-centered learning* (3.01). Thus, the type of training activities currently available to community college faculty in both rural and urban locations focuses strongly on technology implementation, both in the traditional classroom and in the online environment. The impact of the accountability movement by regional and disciplinary accreditation agencies is also reflected in faculty training on issues of student learning assessment. The availability of these programming efforts in both locales indicates a commonality facing faculty across the board.

The survey also asked faculty development leaders to identify which of twenty practices they thought important, even if they did not currently provide for the training. The rationale for this question was to identify gaps in faculty development programming and to begin to predict possible new areas of support for faculty work. The top areas urban and rural faculty development leaders thought important included *offering programming on assessment of student learning* (3.75 and 3.71, respectively), *integrating technology into classroom teaching* (both 3.63), *new faculty development* (3.59 and 3.61, respectively), *teaching underprepared students* (both 3.58), and *student-centered teaching* (3.58 and 3.46, respectively). As indicated earlier, rural and urban campuses are currently offering faculty development programming on assessment of student learning, student-centered teaching, and integration of technology into classroom teaching. However, the level of importance of these programs is relative to the level of current availability; in many cases leaders felt these activities are critical for faculty support but are not offering them to the level they would prefer. Competing demands for resources means that hard choices have to be made; leaders are in fact indicating what is most important to them by what they are currently offering.

Leaders in both rural and urban areas also felt that it is important to offer programming and training on how to teach underprepared students. Programming in this area, however, is limited. Yet the identification of this key need reflects the changing demographics of the community college faculty base, as many instructors retire and the ranks of adjunct faculty are expanded. Providing training to allow adjunct faculty to be most effective in the classroom is also identified by leaders as important. Likewise, the shift in student demographics and the open access admission policies of community colleges results in large percentages of students who enter college requiring remediation. Helping faculty with strategies to work with underprepared students remains an issue that is not currently addressed in programming support for faculty.

For new directions in faculty development, faculty indicated to what extent they thought each of the sixteen new directions listed were now offered, and to what extent they thought the activities should be offered. New directions were identified as those practices with a lesser tradition of programming on campuses. Of note, some of these new direction activities are indeed currently offered at some campuses, but they remain as unfilled programming items for the majority. Of all the items, only one—program assessment—was currently being offered to a moderate extent. Training on program assessment was being offered more often on rural campuses (mean = 3.26) than on urban campuses (mean = 3.07). This result highlights the finding noted previously in this chapter—that rural faculty development leaders equate the importance of institutional and faculty issues, whereas urban developers focus more on individual faculty needs.

Urban and rural development leaders thought a number of activities were important, but they differed about the level of importance of these activities. For example, rural leaders rated program assessment (mean = 3.57, urban mean = 3.41), training for part-time and adjunct faculty (mean = 3.29, urban mean = 3.42), unit or program evaluation (mean = 3.26, urban mean = 3.09), departmental leadership (mean = 3.09, urban mean = 3.11), and support for institutional change priorities (mean = 3.07, urban mean = 3.17). Urban respondents had additional items that they indicated to a moderate extant should be offered. These included ethical conduct of faculty work (mean = 3.07, rural mean = 2.94) and interdisciplinary collaborations (mean = 3.05, rural mean = 2.94). The level of importance for supporting programming for new directions, as represented by the means, was less than that indicated for importance of current practices. Clearly, even though the items for new directions are evident in the literature and identify areas of need for faculty, the factors that guide training efforts coalesce around programming to support instructors' daily practices in the classroom. Thus, the activities to train faculty on effective use of technology in teaching and measuring student learning were more important to developers than new training needs. Rural and urban leaders showed less difference in rating the importance of new directions because these items represented more a desire for the future than an impact on current practice.

Discussion and Conclusion

The portrait presented here illuminates differences and similarities in issues of faculty development in rural and urban community colleges. Currently, development efforts on both rural and urban campuses focus on classroom issues involving both students and the integration of technology and new teaching and learning strategies into classroom teaching. Notably, regardless of location, faculty development leaders believed that they were not currently offering programming at the level they felt they should. Rural developers also supported more institutionally oriented goals, whereas their urban counterparts felt a need for more support for part-time and adjunct faculty. Given the multiple responsibilities of rural administrators, direct links to institutional goals may have been embedded in their administrative function. Thus, helping faculty meet departmental and institutional goals may accomplish a multitude of purposes. Although urban colleges supported institutional goals, they also noted a need to support part-time faculty. Part-time faculty are more prevalent in urban than in rural areas; thus, this choice is likely linked to institutional context.

The location of the community college in a rural or urban area showed the most impact when the items identified as faculty and institutional challenges were reviewed. More agreement was found in the responses from urban developers; that is, larger percentages of respondents indicated an item as one of the top three challenges facing faculty and the institution. Rural colleges focused more on institutional issues of departmental leadership and training future faculty because they employ more full-time faculty and the pool from which departmental leaders are drawn is smaller. Urban colleges noted greater challenges in dealing with multicultural issues and shifting student demographics. This may be because rural areas tend to be more homogenous in their populations, and given their isolated locations, have not witnessed an influx of students of color. The lack of student diversity in rural locations creates a different institutional issue—one not necessarily addressed by development efforts.

The research reported here has several implications. First, faculty developers in both urban and rural areas do not rely on professional organizations to support faculty development efforts. Associations might consider providing programming in a regional format in order to reach a wider variety of community college faculty developers. As well, because many community college administrators make decisions about development efforts based on their previous experience as faculty, it is important that those leading faculty development efforts have a wide breadth of experience utilizing faculty development programming and are knowledgeable about the critical issues facing faculty today. Rural faculty developers' concerns about preparing future faculty points to issues raised in another chapter in this volume—namely, the use of more full-time faculty in rural areas and the challenges of faculty recruitment and retention (see Chapter Six).

Recruitment and retention of faculty at rural community college campuses can be enhanced with a structure in place to support faculty development. Because community colleges value teaching, programming to support faculty in acquiring the skills to effectively use technology in teaching and working with underprepared students becomes increasingly important. Community college faculty are trained in their disciplines, with few having education on teaching pedagogy or working with the wide span of students at two-year colleges that include high school dual enrollments, traditional college students, and adult learners. In rural areas, the community college is often the only provider of training for faculty, whereas in urban areas community college faculty members have university programs, professional development workshops, and access to other teaching resources and support. Thus, it becomes more critical for rural community colleges to provide an infrastructure for faculty development. Rural development leaders may enhance their programming efforts by calling on other institutional units to provide training or by working with local public school systems to collaborate on programming opportunities by pooling resources.

Both rural and urban community college efforts to support faculty on their campuses point to the changing and expanding nature of faculty roles. As these institutions position themselves to face the challenges of both resource constraints and increased public demand for an inexpensive education, it is critical to have faculty who are prepared to face these shifting demands, and for institutions to consider how faculty development efforts can aid in achieving institutional change priorities. As noted, faculty developers do not believe they are offering the level of programming that they feel they need to. In the end, Faustian bargains are struck, and campus leaders provide the training they believe to be most critical despite larger needs. The fact that rural developers noted a focus on programming that also supports institutional goals means that faculty development is recognized as a key to the college's success.

Collaborations between urban and rural community colleges could provide a way to leverage funding to provide an expanded forum of programming for faculty. Sharing resources and networking on best practices would serve as a win-win for both institutions. Regional or statewide faculty development programming could allow for the pooling of resources to make available a wider array of programming. Internet-based training is another, more frequent training resource in rural areas. As noted in Chapter Nine, however, Internet connection remains limited at some colleges in remote areas. Professional associations could also target programming on a state level to increase access to training opportunities. Central to the efforts in all community colleges is preparing faculty to better serve students.

References

Centra, J. *Faculty Development Practices in U.S. Colleges and Universities.* Project Report 76–30. Princeton, N.J.: Princeton Educational Testing Service, 1976.

Cohen, A. M., and Brawer, F. B. *The American Community College.* (4th ed.) San Francisco: Jossey-Bass, 2003.

Erickson, G. "A Survey of Faculty Development Practices." In M. Svinicki (ed.), *To Improve the Academy.* Stillwater, Okla.: New Forums Press, 1986.

Murray, J. P. "Faculty Development in Publicly Supported Two-Year Colleges." *Community College Journal of Research and Practice,* 2001, *25,* 487–502.

Murray, J. P. "Meeting the Needs of New Faculty at Rural Community Colleges." *Community College Journal of Research and Practice,* 2005, *29,* 215–232.

Sorcinelli, M. D., Austin, A. E., Eddy, P. L., and Beach, A. L. *Creating the Future of Faculty Development: Learning from the Past, Understanding the Present.* Bolton, Mass.: Anker, 2006.

VanderStaay, S. L. "In the Right Direction." *Chronicle of Higher Education,* June 10, 2005, p. B5.

Wolfe, J. R., and Strange, C. C. "Academic Life at the Franchise: Faculty Culture in a Rural Two-Year Branch Campus." *Review of Higher Education,* 2003, 26(3), 343–362.

PAMELA L. EDDY *is associate professor of higher education and doctoral program coordinator in education leadership at Central Michigan University.*

Although most community colleges do not have on-campus housing, many rural two-year colleges do. Relying on federal institutional survey data, this chapter discusses issues related to the operation of residence halls and implications for both students and rural community college leaders. The chapter concludes with recommendations for policy and practice.

Residential Living at Rural Community Colleges

Pat G. Moeck, David E. Hardy, Stephen G. Katsinas

In a feature article about how budget cuts affect different types of institutions, Travis J. Reindl (as cited in Hebel, 2003), director of state policy analysis for the American Association of State Colleges and Universities, argued that budget cuts have a more severe impact on four-year public institutions, because "regional universities have fixed costs, such as heating dormitories, that community colleges do not face" (p. 22). Embedded in Reindl's assertion is a common myth about community colleges—that none of them are residential institutions.

Yet in 2005 an analysis of 2001–02 data from the U.S. Department of Education's Integrated Postsecondary Education Data System (IPEDS) found that 232 of the nation's 1,163 institutions classified by NCES as public two-year institutions offered on-campus student housing. Using the 2005 Basic Classifications for Institutions of Higher Education from the Carnegie Foundation for the Advancement of Teaching, 190 of these 232 institutions are classified as rural associate degree–granting colleges. Together, these 190 colleges served an estimated 39,000 students in the 2001–02 academic year, and produced an average of $258,000 in annual institutional revenue from on-campus housing (Moeck, 2005). This chapter begins with a discussion of the limited literature regarding community college housing and then

The authors wish to thank J. Mark Leech for his assistance in the preparation of this chapter.

reviews the context of residential housing on rural community college campuses. This chapter concludes with a discussion of the implications of residential living for two-year colleges.

Literature on Residential Community Colleges

Although there is extensive literature on a wide variety of issues related to the advantages, disadvantages, management, administration, and operation of on-campus housing for students, this literature is almost exclusively related to on-campus housing at four-year institutions. In their work *How College Affects Students: A Third Decade of Research,* Pascarella and Terenzini (2005, p. 603) synthesize several studies of on-campus housing, and conclude:

> Living on campus (versus living off campus or commuting) was the single most consistent within-college determinant of the impact of college. Net of important background traits and other confounding influences, living on campus had statistically significant, positive impacts on increases in aesthetic, cultural, and intellectual values; liberalization of social, political, and religious values and attitudes; development of more positive self-concepts; intellectual orientation, autonomy, and independence; tolerance, empathy, and ability to relate to others' and the use of principled reasoning to judge moral issues. Residing on campus also significantly increased the likelihood of persisting in college and earning a bachelor's degree. In addition, residing in an on-campus living-learning center bolstered the positive influence on persistence. Little evidence, however, suggested that living on or off campus influenced either knowledge acquisition or general cognitive growth. Living on campus, however, appears to foster change indirectly, by maximizing the opportunities for social, cultural, and extracurricular engagement.

Virtually every housing study reviewed in *How College Affects Students* addresses housing in the context of four-year colleges and universities. Pascarella and Terenzini's (1991, 2005) research implies that the same benefits would translate to students at residential community colleges, but to date this population of students has not been specifically studied in what could be considered to be an extensive or meaningful way.

A review of the literature found just three relevant studies of on-campus housing at American community colleges. The first was a survey of the members of the American Association of Community and Junior Colleges' Rural-Small Colleges Commission, which was created in the early 1980s and discontinued in 1992. This 1988 survey by Summers and Budig of Vincennes University, at the time a two-year college in Indiana, reported the results of a survey of chief executive officers at 244 community colleges, of which roughly a third (77) operated residence halls. Most residence halls were found to be at community colleges located in the southeastern United States and in areas with low population density. The housing offered was coed, with approximately five hundred beds per institution. About half of the 77 colleges (38) offered housing specifically for student athletes, one-fifth (17) offered dedicated married student housing, and one-eighth (12) offered housing specifically for international students. Summer conference housing was offered by 70 of the 77 respondents, and half (36 of 77) offered tutoring services in their housing units (Summers and Budig, 1988).

Two doctoral dissertation studies concerning housing at community colleges have also been conducted. Catt (1998) used a qualitative interview data collection methodology and found that student success and retention was directly proportional to the number of on-campus residence halls offered by the college and used by students. Catt's study focused primarily on student development theory and how such theory translated into attitudes and policies that enable students to learn. The second dissertation, by Doggett (1981), represented an attempt to learn whether or not community colleges had a cogent philosophy related to the role of residence halls in student education and student development. Finding that such a philosophy did not generally exist at community colleges, Doggett attempted to develop his own philosophy based on the qualitative and quantitative data he collected. By analyzing survey data collected from presidents of community colleges accredited by the Southern Association of Colleges and Schools' Commission on Colleges, Doggett's proposed "residence hall philosophy" suggested that community colleges that engage in the operation of on-campus housing needed to ensure that they have specific goals and objectives related to the role of the residence halls in student development and education, have a method to ensure that qualified staff were selected for the management and operation of campus housing, and design and deliver specific programming that would assist students in their intellectual and personal development.

Building on these studies, Moeck (2005) adapted Summers and Budig's (1988) survey instrument, adding questions designed to examine issues related to residential life at community colleges with on-campus housing. The survey was distributed to all 232 community colleges that reported housing to IPEDS, of which 190 were classified as rural according to the 2005 Carnegie Basic Classifications. One hundred and seventeen of the 190 rural colleges returned usable responses, for a response rate of 62 percent. The following sections discuss the results of Moeck's (2005) survey and discuss implications for practice and policy.

Location of Community Colleges with Residential Housing

Where are the colleges that report residential housing for students located? Of the 232 associate degree–granting institutions that reported residential housing to IPEDS, 206 are classified by the 2005 Carnegie Basic Classifications as public stand-alone, associate degree–granting colleges; the remaining 28 are classified as public associate degree–granting, two-year colleges

NEW DIRECTIONS FOR COMMUNITY COLLEGES • DOI: 10.1002/cc

operated by 4-year universities. Thus, the great majority, 190 of 206, or 93 percent, of public community colleges with residential housing facilities are classified by Carnegie as rural. Among the 206 publicly controlled community colleges reporting residential housing, 51 (25 percent) are classified by the Carnegie 2005 Basic Classifications as small rural colleges, 107 (52 percent) as medium rural colleges, and 32 (16 percent) as large rural colleges. Thus, residential housing is most common at medium rural-serving colleges, although this finding must be tempered by the underreporting problem described in the following sections, which likely affects smaller institutions.

Of the 117 responses to Moeck's 2005 survey of rural community colleges, 27 (23 percent) were small rural institutions, 75 (64 percent) were medium rural institutions, and 15 (13 percent) were large rural colleges. This distribution is fairly representative of the universe of rural community colleges that offer on-campus housing with a slight overrepresentation of medium rural community colleges and a slight underrepresentation of small and large rural institutions.

By accrediting region, the North Central Association of Colleges and Schools accredit 46 percent of the rural community colleges that responded to Moeck's survey. Another 32 percent are accredited by the Southern Association of Colleges and Schools; these are the two largest regional accrediting agencies. Thus, by region, 78 percent of the rural community colleges offering on-campus housing are located in the South, Midwest, and Great Plains.

Types of Housing and Services Offered in Residence Halls at Rural Community Colleges

This section describes specific types of housing and services commonly provided at rural community colleges with residential housing in order to guide practitioners who may be considering building or expanding residential life at their institutions. As Table 8.1 illustrates, rural community colleges offer an array of specialized types of housing. The most common type of specialized or dedicated residential housing is housing designated specifically for athletes. Of the 117 usable responses, 34 (29 percent) colleges offer housing for student athletes. This finding parallels Castañeda's (2004) assertion that there are a total of 73,936 student athletes at community colleges, of whom just fewer than 60 percent are enrolled at rural community colleges. Using the same typology, Castañeda found that 38 percent of all American community colleges had athletic departments, of which 54 percent were rural colleges. Based on these findings, it is fairly likely that many athletic scholarships at community colleges include room and board. The higher percentages of full-time male students enrolled at rural institutions may reflect the higher number of student athletes (Hardy, 2005).

Of the 117 institutions that responded, 33 (28 percent) indicated private rooms were available at their institutions. Although the choices are likely more limited in many rural areas, more and more students are demanding pri-

Table 8.1. Types of Student Housing Offered at Rural Community Colleges

| Type of Housing | Rural Colleges Offering This Type of Housing (Number) | Responding Rural Colleges Offering This Type of Housing (Percent) | Type of Rural Community College | | |
			Small	Medium	Large
Athletics residence	34	29	8	18	8
Private rooms	33	28	8	19	6
Twelve-month/year-round	28	24	4	20	4
Single parent/family	23	20	4	17	2
Married student/family	17	15	4	12	1
Specific academic program	15	13	3	10	2
Honors	12	10	1	8	3
Quiet or intensive study	10	9	3	7	0
First year experience	5	4	1	3	1
International house	4	3	1	2	1

Note: Percentages based on a total of 117 usable responses from rural community colleges.

vate, personal space in residence halls. Residential housing for single parents and families, as well as married students and their families, was offered by 23 (20 percent) and 17 (15 percent), respectively, of the responding rural colleges. In addition, 15 rural colleges (13 percent) offered residential housing for specific academic programs. It is probable that these two patterns—availability of family housing and availability of housing for students in particular academic pursuits—are related. The colleges may offer specialized programs in allied health and nursing, first responder training, or engineering technology, and use residential housing as a recruitment tool. For example, North Central Texas College's rural Gainesville campus offers housing for married students with children, which in turn supports enrollments in their nursing and allied health programs. Itasca Community College in northeast Minnesota has developed a cluster college model for its Engineering Technology program, and has constructed two residence halls in recent years. In addition, 12 rural colleges reported offering honors residential housing, another sign that these colleges are committed to serving traditional-age students.

In addition, although this is not surprising given the year-round nature of most community college curricular offerings, 24 percent (28) of the responding rural community colleges offer twelve-month residence hall contracts. For students who attend classes year-round, who practice with their athletic teams during summers and breaks, or who work at twelve-month jobs on campus or in the vicinity, year-round living accommodations are of critical importance. Moeck (2005) concluded that by offering specialized housing segmented to different student markets, rural community colleges can extend their programs and services and become more student-centered. This result is consistent with the findings of Catt (1998) and Doggett (1981), who qualitatively interviewed students and recorded their preferences in housing services.

As rural community colleges approach entering the housing market, it is important to consider the residential services that are being made available to attract and retain students. The most common services for students in on-campus housing at rural colleges are laundry facilities (85 percent), in-room cable TV (81 percent), and telephone service (80 percent). The high frequency of these amenities indicates that these services are expected as part of the residential college experience. The increasing availability of cell phones and reduction of "dead space" in more sparsely populated areas of rural America may explain why landline telephone service was slightly less popular than laundry facilities and cable TV.

For rural community college practitioners considering building or expanding their residential life services, it is important to think about how to integrate learning technologies into on-campus living spaces. Respondents from rural colleges reported that 67 percent of the campuses provided students with access to computers in their living quarters; this is not surprising given the technology demands and expectations of incoming college students. The provision of computer access indicates that community college leaders are listening to and accommodating their students' desires to write, surf the Web, conduct research, send e-mails, play computer games, listen to music, and perform other basic computer functions from their own personal residence hall spaces. As more instructors rely on the Internet for testing, research assignments, and chat room discussions as required components of their courses, computer access from the residence halls will likely increase in importance and may become a marketing tool to fill residence halls.

Fitness centers (52 percent), in-hall tutoring (50 percent), nonsmoking rooms (50 percent), and access control systems to promote safety (36 percent) are also commonly available in on-campus residences at rural community colleges. It should be noted that just because tutoring is not available at the residence hall does not mean it is not easily accessible in another nearby building on campus, such as a student services center. In this same vein, an on-campus gymnasium open to students for extended hours could be considered a fitness center in addition to the smaller residence hall–based fitness rooms that are similar to fitness rooms found at apartment complexes or small hotels.

Demographically, the typical student living in on-campus housing at a rural community college is of traditional college age (eighteen to twenty-four), unmarried, male, and taking a full course load. At small rural colleges, 60 percent of students living on campus are male. Males make up 56 percent of students living on campus at medium rural colleges, and 54 percent of those at large rural colleges. The percentages of males in the residence halls is higher than the national averages of males enrolled in small, medium, and large rural community colleges, where they account for 43, 42, and 45 percent, respectively, of the student body (Hardy, 2005). According to Moeck (2005), although the survey data does not demonstrate how much athletics contributes to on-campus housing at rural community colleges, it might help explain why the percentage of males living on campus at community colleges is so much greater than their proportion in the general rural community college student population. Furthermore, more than 67 percent of students at small rural colleges, 73 percent of those attending medium-size rural colleges, and 64 percent of students at large rural community colleges are enrolled in transfer, as opposed to vocational, curricula. Given the smaller economic base in rural areas, vocational jobs are less plentiful. Students desiring more educational options may enroll in transfer programs to equip themselves with a wider skill base and more career choices.

Motivation of Rural Community Colleges Operating Residential Housing

For rural community college leaders involved with the administration of residential housing, commitment to reducing geographic barriers to access is the top reason why their colleges offer on-campus housing. Residential housing allows the college to serve students who live a long distance from the campus. Rural community colleges also offer housing in order to increase the number of full-time enrollments and to attract minority students and student athletes. In addition, the student services offered to full-time residential students become accessible to commuter students who attend on either a full- or part-time basis. For these institutions, then, residential housing allows them to offer a collegiate experience that includes a broad mix of programs and services that otherwise would be unavailable (Moeck, 2005).

Rural community colleges may also choose to provide on-campus housing to support student development activities such as clubs, organizations, teams, and other student groups. These programs and services may make a difference in student recruitment, retention, and overall satisfaction with their education (Moeck, 2005). Feeling that they are a part of a community college is a fundamental need for a large number of first-time college students, and may be a strong factor leading to student success (Pascarella and Terenzini, 2005). In addition, when student leaders live on campus, they are more available to members of their organizations, faculty sponsors, administrators, and other interested parties (Catt, 1998). Unlike the commuter student who must drive twenty-five miles to attend classes, a student who resides in a residence hall can participate easily in engagement-engendering activities such as clubs and student organizations.

For community colleges interested in the residential life market, it is important to consider issues of organization, administration, and finances. Most respondents indicated that the operation of on-campus residence halls falls under the purview of the institution's student affairs division. The most common titles of the community college's chief housing officer are director of housing, dean of student services, and director of student life. Usually, two people are involved in the administration of the housing unit on the campus, and each of them often wears other administrative hats as well—a common practice at many rural community colleges. Four-fifths of the rural community colleges that responded to this survey (this proportion is steady across small, medium-size, and large rural colleges) indicated that their residence halls were filled to capacity, and thirty-two noted that they had wait lists.

Respondents were also asked how much money was generated by their on-campus residence halls, but only a small percentage of respondents answered this question. Of the thirty-two that did respond, the average revenue generated from on-campus housing exceeded $1 million per year. Considering that the average total current funds revenues for all small, medium-size, and large rural-serving colleges reporting to IPEDS in 2000–01 was approximately $10 million, $20 million, and $48 million, respectively (Hardy, 2005), this may be highly significant. For small rural colleges, housing revenues may make up 10 percent of total current funds revenues. The importance of this quasi-unrestricted revenue stream is underscored by studies that document a lack of unrestricted funds for internal entrepreneurial activities at these smaller colleges (Katsinas, Alexander, and Opp, 2003), against a backdrop of a long-term decline of state appropriations for community colleges between 1981 and 2001 (Roessler, 2005). This significant revenue stream may explain why half of the rural community colleges responding to this survey indicated that their institutions were considering constructing new housing (Moeck, 2005). Rural community colleges may also be motivated to construct new dorms in order to provide affordable housing for their students. For example, Schweitzer (2006) reports that Greenfield Community College, a suburban community college in Massachusetts, is currently constructing housing specifically for single parents. Greenfield's president noted that many students who lack affordable housing work too many hours and this affects their studies. For students in rural areas who are trying to juggle work, family, and college responsibilities, and who now also struggle with higher gas prices in areas where publicly subsidized mass transportation rarely exists, on-campus housing may be particularly appealing.

Conclusion

As this chapter demonstrates, a large percentage of community colleges offer on-campus housing, and most residential community colleges are located in rural areas. It is important to note that the number of colleges offering residential housing may be underrepresented in the IPEDS data. The authors together have visited more than three hundred community colleges in thirty-five states over the past two decades, and have observed firsthand that many rural community colleges have residence halls. Indeed, anecdotal data and information gleaned from college Web sites and discussions with college leaders in several states lead us to believe that the total number of community colleges with on-campus housing may well be double the number reported to IPEDS. Given the obvious student life, recruitment, and retention benefits—not to mention the financial benefits to the institutions at a time of fiscal strain—we expect colleges in other states will follow the lead of the institutions described in Minnesota, Massachusetts, and Texas and construct on-campus residence halls in the future. In doing so, many of the special needs of students at these unique institutions can be successfully met.

Community college leaders will need to contemplate the advantages and challenges of implementing housing options for students. Student development researchers (Pascarella and Terenzini, 2005) conclude that cocurricular activities provide unique learning opportunities for students and aid in student retention. Certainly, residential housing provides additional opportunities for student programming to develop an enhanced learning experience. However, residential housing also presents both fiscal and student challenges. Upkeep of resident halls and the balance of profitability of housing need to be considered. Additional student issues may evolve when students are on campus, including alcohol abuse and safety issues. As leaders in rural areas weigh the individual benefits and costs of residential housing, they can be assured that other community colleges do indeed provide living quarters for students.

References

Castañeda, C. "A National Overview of Intercollegiate Athletics in Public Community Colleges." Unpublished doctoral dissertation, University of North Texas, 2004.

Catt, S. "Adjustment Problems of Freshmen Attending a Distant, Non-Residential Community College." Unpublished doctoral dissertation, University of Pittsburgh, 1998.

Doggett, B. "A Study to Develop Guidelines for Enhancing Student Development Through Residence Education in Community Colleges." Unpublished doctoral dissertation, East Texas State University, 1981.

Hardy, D. E. "A Two-Year College Typology for the 21st Century: Updating and Utilizing the Katsinas-Lacey Classification System." Unpublished doctoral dissertation, University of North Texas, 2005.

Hebel, S. "Unequal Impact." *Chronicle of Higher Education*, 2003, 49(38), A21–A22.

Katsinas, S. G., Alexander, K. F., and Opp, R. D. *Preserving Access with Excellence: Financing for Rural Community Colleges*. Rural Community College Initiative Policy Paper. Chapel Hill, N.C.: MDC, Inc., 2003.

Moeck, P. G. "An Analysis of On-Campus Housing at Public Rural Community Colleges in the United States." Unpublished doctoral dissertation, University of North Texas, 2005.

Pascarella, E. T., and Terenzini, P. T. *How College Affects Students: Findings and Insights from Twenty Years of Research*. San Francisco: Jossey-Bass, 1991.

Pascarella, E. T., and Terenzini, P. T. *How College Affects Students: A Third Decade of Research*. San Francisco: Jossey-Bass, 2005.

Roessler, B. C. "A Quantitative Study of Revenues and Expenditures at U.S. Community Colleges, 1980–2001." Unpublished doctoral dissertation, University of North Texas, Denton, 2005.

Schweitzer, S. "Community Colleges Seek to Build Dorms: Reflects Changing Student Profile at Three State Schools." *Boston Globe.* 2006, Feb. 26. http://www.boston.com/news/local/articles/2006/02/19/community_colleges_seek_to_build_dorms/. Accessed Nov. 21, 2006.

Summers, P., and Budig, J. "Residence Hall Systems at Community and Junior Colleges." Paper presented at the annual convention of the American Association of Community and Junior Colleges, Las Vegas, Apr. 1988.

PAT G. MOECK is program director of the Medical Assisting Program at El Centro College, Dallas County Community College District.

DAVID E. HARDY is assistant professor of higher education and director of research for the Education Policy Center at the University of Alabama.

STEPHEN G. KATSINAS is director of the Education Policy Center and professor of higher education at the University of Alabama.

9

This chapter reviews the literature on the status of distance education in rural community colleges, and addresses issues rural community colleges face in implementing distance education.

Connecting to the Larger World: Distance Education in Rural Community Colleges

Brent D. Cejda

With their reputation for responsiveness, adaptability, and flexibility, one could easily assume that community colleges would lead the way in implementing and refining distance education offerings. Data from the U.S. Department of Education support this assumption. In the 2000–01 academic year, 90 percent (960 of 1,070) of public two-year colleges offered 55,900 courses through various types of distance education (U.S. Department of Education, 2002). This percentage is only slightly higher than at public four-year institutions, where during the same year 89 percent (550 of 620) offered courses through distance education. Total enrollments in distance education courses at community colleges, however, represent 61 percent of total distance education offerings by both public two- and four-year institutions.

In the mid-1990s, distance education was viewed as the future for rural community colleges (MacBrayne, 1995). Sink and Jackson (2000), however, were among the first to point to a "digital divide" between urban and rural community colleges. The authors found that urban community colleges were often better wired than their rural counterparts, preventing the rural institutions from providing their students with the same level of access to technological resources. Based on data from government reports, Katsinas and Moeck (2002) concluded that the urban and rural divide was actually widening. This chapter reviews literature on the status of distance education in rural community colleges, examining in particular whether there has been a narrowing of the digital divide.

NEW DIRECTIONS FOR COMMUNITY COLLEGES, no. 137, Spring 2007 © 2007 Wiley Periodicals, Inc.
Published online in Wiley InterScience (www.interscience.wiley.com) • DOI: 10.1002/cc.273

The Internet in Rural Areas

As shown in Table 9.1, fewer rural residents use the Internet than suburban and urban residents. This disparity in usage remained constant between 2000 and 2003. A more recent survey (Horrigan and Murray, 2006) indicates that the gap has decreased to 8 percent, with 52 percent penetration in rural communities and 60 percent penetration in suburban and urban communities. An obvious question is whether community type influences Internet usage. Statistical analyses indicate little or no influence related to rural residence and Internet usage (Bell, Reddy, and Rainie, 2004). Of those that use the Internet, rural residents are online as much or more than suburban or urban residents. Thus, there appear to be other explanations of the differences in Internet penetration.

Some of the differences between Internet usage in rural areas and other locations can be explained by demographics such as age, income levels, and educational attainment (Bell, Reddy, and Rainie, 2004). Younger adults (eighteen to forty-nine years of age) are more likely to use the Internet than are older adults (fifty or older). A greater percentage of rural communities (46 percent) are made up of older adults, in comparison to suburban (38 percent) and urban (36 percent) communities. Internet usage also rises as income rises, yet almost one-half (47 percent) of the American households earning under $30,000 a year are in rural areas. Furthermore, Internet usage increases with educational attainment through the baccalaureate degree. However, rural communities contain higher percentages of residents (59 percent) who have not completed high school or who hold a high school degree as their highest educational degree, compared to residents of suburban (43 percent) and urban (44 percent) communities.

Two other factors also explain why Internet penetration is lower in rural areas. First, a greater number of rural residents indicate that they have fewer choices about how they can access the Internet. Results from Bell, Reddy, and Rainie's (2004) survey indicate that almost 29 percent of rural Internet users have only one Internet Service Provider (ISP) for their locale. Suburban and urban Internet users have more choices; more than 90 percent have multiple ISPs. Second, as shown in Table 9.1, less than one-fourth of rural residents have broadband connection. Although overall Internet penetration has increased, there is still a digital divide in broadband connection and therefore in the use of broadband applications.

According to Wu and Turner (2006), the difference between narrowband and broadband Internet access is the amount of time it takes for data transfer and the type of data that can be transferred. Narrowband, or "dial-up" Internet access, is slower than broadband access where connection occurs through sources such as digital subscriber line (DSL), cable modem, satellite, and optical fiber. An advantage of broadband is the ability to receive larger files and real-time audio and video transfer. From the perspective of distance education, broadband access becomes important when the

Table 9.1. Internet Penetration and Broadband Connection in the United States

Community Type	Percentage Internet Penetration (Broadband Connection)					
	2000	2001	2002	2003	2004	2005
Urban communities	51 (N/A)	62 (9)	58 (18)	67 (21)	N/A (29)	N/A (38)
Suburban communities	55 (N/A)	62 (9)	63 (17)	66 (23)	N/A (29)	N/A (40)
Rural communities	41 (N/A)	50 (3)	49 (6)	52 (9)	N/A (16)	N/A (24)

Source: Bell, Reddy, and Rainie (2004).

design of a class involves the use of audio and video sources, or when instructor-to-learner or learner-to-learner interaction is a component. Narrowband access remains viable in distance education situations where the learner needs only gain access to text-based information.

It is not clear why fewer rural residents have broadband connections than individuals living in urban and suburban areas. Is it that a broadband connection is not available, or is it because broadband is available but not used? Bell, Reddy, and Rainie (2004) report that 25 percent of rural Internet users do not believe a high-speed connection to their home is available. As well, a recent broadcast of *All Things Considered* on National Public Radio (Block, 2005) pointed out that broadband access might be available in rural towns, but not in homes located outside of those towns. Similarly, a report by the Free Press (2005) stressed that the monthly fees for broadband access in rural areas are too expensive. The issue of cost is not a new one. In 1995, Bill Gates warned of the expense involved in extending broadband wiring to remote communities and homes. He suggested applying the doctrine of universal service to the "information highway," providing funding for Internet access in the same manner that rural mail, telephone, and electrical services have been subsidized. More recently, Glass, Talluto, and Babb (2003) have argued that providing access through technologies such as DSL extenders and wireless connections would cost less than upgrading the multimillion miles of rural telephone lines that are not yet broadband-capable.

Distance Education Technologies

Distance education is not a new term or phenomenon. Early versions of distance education included correspondence courses and live instruction at off-campus sites. In the last decade, however, distance education has become linked almost universally with the Internet. Kinley (2001) found that "today's distance education focus has dramatically shifted toward network-based technologies (in general) and Internet-based delivery (more specifically)" (p. 7). Today, community colleges use the Internet more than other technology-based delivery strategies, such as interactive audio, video, or compact disc, and the use of technology is rapidly replacing correspondence and live instructors who go on the road to deliver classes in rural locations (Waits and Lewis, 2003). Based on the shift to technology-based delivery, Burnell (2002) defines distance learning "simply as an instruction and learning practice, utilizing technology and involving students and teachers who are separated by time and space" (p. 4).

Among distance education technologies employed by public community colleges, Internet delivery has become dominant. The U.S. Department of Education reports that 95 percent of public community colleges use asynchronous Internet—defined as not simultaneous—as the primary technology for instructional delivery in distance offerings (Waits and Lewis, 2003). The second-most popular distance technology is two-way audio or visual, used by 60 percent of the reporting institutions. Recognizing the need to gather information on the use of Internet delivery in higher education, the Sloan Consortium began an annual survey of online education in 2003. Although the consortium reports do not look at the same specific factors longitudinally, the findings illustrate the tremendous growth in the use of the Internet to deliver distance education courses.

The Sloan Consortium's initial report (Allen and Seaman, 2003) revealed that in fall 2002, almost 11 percent of the students attending two-year colleges enrolled in at least one online course. The consortium's second report (Allen and Seaman, 2004) noted that in fall 2003, almost half of all students enrolled in online education were attending two-year colleges. The most recent report (Allen and Seaman, 2005) found that slightly more than three-fourths (77.5 percent) of two-year colleges use the Internet to offer courses that are applicable to degrees, and more than two-thirds (70.8 percent) use the Internet to offer continuing education or noncredit courses. In addition, 39.8 percent of the institutions offering regular, face-to-face associate degrees also offer at least one online degree program. Although the Sloan Consortium's surveys do not present information on course and program offerings by geographical location, they demonstrate that in the past three years community colleges have embraced the Internet as a primary means of providing distance education.

A study of Internet-based offerings in career and technical education (CTE) at community colleges (Johnson and others, 2004) did examine information based on geographic location. This study included a random sample of 512 member institutions of the American Association of Community Colleges. Among the 270 responding institutions, greater percentages of community colleges in urban (82.8 percent) and suburban (80.5 percent) settings offered Internet-based courses than in rural (66.3 percent) communities. The primary difference between the findings of this study and the Sloan surveys is the reported percentages of credit and noncredit courses delivered via the Internet. Johnson and others report that rural community colleges offer 71.9 percent of their credit and 48.4 percent of their noncredit continuing education courses via the Internet. Within these overall figures, the percentages for rural institutions do not differ significantly from the percentages offered for urban and suburban colleges.

It is important to examine the more than 20 percentage-point difference in noncredit distance offerings noted in the most recent Sloan Consortium report (Allen and Seaman, 2005) and the career and technical education (CTE) study (Johnson and others, 2004). This difference may reflect a disparity in the types of distance offerings, because the Sloan report includes all types of noncredit offerings (basic skills, GED, personal development, and enrichment) whereas the CTE study focuses only on noncredit offerings applicable to career and technical education. Epper and Garn (2003) point to the common perception that the overwhelming majority of distance education offerings are general rather than vocational. The CTE study also suggests that fewer institution-developed vocational courses are offered by rural community colleges; according to Johnson and others, 17.9 percent of the rural institutions offered CTE Internet-based courses developed by commercial vendors and 23.2 percent offered CTE Internet-based courses in partnership with other colleges and universities. To date, the majority of reports and studies have collected information on how many community colleges provide Internet-based offerings. The disparity in these sources indicates the need to also gather information on the types of offerings.

A survey of 125 chief academic officers at rural community colleges in the states of Arkansas, Arizona, Colorado, Louisiana, New Mexico, Oklahoma, Texas, Utah, and Wyoming (Cejda, forthcoming) provides information on the types of technology used in distance education and the curriculum offered through distance education. The survey asked questions about the percentage of academic transfer and vocational or occupational curricula that was delivered using the Internet or other forms of distance technology. Ninety-three percent of the respondents reported that less than 25 percent of the academic transfer curriculum was delivered through online instruction, and 86.1 percent reported that fewer than 25 percent of these courses were delivered through other distance technologies. Similarly, 97.1 percent of the respondents reported that fewer than 25 percent of their vocational courses were delivered through online instruction, and 94.3 percent reported that less than 25 percent of their vocational curriculum was delivered through other distance technologies. Less than 2 percent of the respondents offered 75 percent or more of either curriculum through all distance technologies. In simple terms, the rural institutions that responded to this survey are using distance technologies to deliver a few courses rather than complete programs.

One particular response to survey questions about technology issues provides insight into why Internet use lags behind other forms of distance education at rural community colleges. Student access to computers emerged as the most pressing technology issue for these rural community colleges, reported by 93.6 percent of chief academic officers. This need for access implies that at rural colleges it is not common for students to own computers and that the institutions are struggling to provide widespread access for their student population. Distance education via the Internet is based on the premise that there is a sufficient population who own personal computers.

Research about distance education offered by rural community colleges is limited. There is initial evidence, however, that rural institutions lag behind their urban and suburban counterparts in terms of the percentage offering Internet-based courses. In addition, it appears that rural community colleges are using distance technologies to offer only a small portion of their curricula, rather than complete certificate or degree programs. Beyond concerns about Internet access and broadband connection, rural community colleges continue to wrestle with fundamental technology issues. In addition to the access-to-computers issue, the technological competence of faculty and students rank among the other top technology issues at rural community colleges (Cejda, forthcoming). In other words, rural community colleges face a spectrum of challenges related to developing and implementing distance education technologies.

Developing and Implementing Distance Education Programs in Rural Community Colleges

Although the potential to expand or enhance offerings through distance technology is obvious, experts stress the need to carefully consider the difference between this opportunity and an institution's capacity to pursue the opportunity. Gallagher (2002) uses the community college to illustrate capacity issues. He points out that community colleges have made significant efforts to provide academic support for students, so they are more likely to have the capacity to provide this support using distance technologies. However, community colleges may not have as great a capacity for providing faculty training for distance technologies or for providing student services through distance technologies. Educators must undertake a comprehensive examination of an institution's capacity to develop the infrastructure necessary to deliver instruction online, provide student and faculty support, and offer program administration. As well, community college leaders must take the necessary steps to develop capacity in these areas if they are to ensure successful implementation of distance programming.

The concept of capacity—the ability to do something—emerges time and again in the literature on distance education. Developing the faculty's technological capacity to provide distance instruction appears to be a key component in successful distance programs. O'Quinn and Corry (2002) found that faculty were often reluctant to participate in distance education because they did not have and were sometimes overwhelmed by the expertise required to develop and deliver a course in this manner. Roberson and Klotz (2002) pointed to a lack of institutional support as one reason why faculty are reluctant to develop and teach online courses. However, Kinley (2001) emphasizes that, as with any instructional matter, faculty buy-in is crucial to any initiative. Support from the top level of the administration is necessary to gain faculty buy-in and provide the necessary institutional capacity to support faculty as they acquire the skills to develop and implement distance education programs.

An emphasis on faculty capacity from the human resources perspective may be even more important in rural community colleges. For example, 68 percent of two-year colleges report that their online classes are taught primarily by full-time faculty (Allen and Seaman, 2005). Rural community colleges do not commonly have a large pool of qualified adjuncts to draw from. Without a large number of part-time instructors, faculty capacity to offer distance education turns into a decision based on costs. Providing release time to initiate or expand distance programs removes a full-time faculty member from the classroom, and if an adjunct is not available, fewer credit hours will be generated. Not all rural institutions are able to justify this cost.

The community colleges actively involved in distance education are not alone in their efforts. Eighty-three percent of public two-year institutions participate in a distance education consortium (Waits and Lewis, 2003). Of those involved in a consortium, it is most common to participate in a state (87 percent) or district (49 percent) consortium. Less common are regional (9 percent), national (6 percent), and international (2 percent) consortia. As reported earlier, curricula developed by commercial vendors have also been used to provide distance programming. Partnerships with other educational entities and the use of commercial products are possible solutions for rural community colleges that are just beginning distance efforts or for those that wish to expand programming but have institutional or faculty capacity limitations.

The Wyoming Community College Distance Education Consortium (WyDEC, 2004) provides an example of an effort to meet the growing demand for distance education in a state that is predominately rural. The consortium includes representatives from the seven Wyoming community colleges, the University of Wyoming, Wyoming Public Television, and the Wyoming Community College Commission. WyDEC serves as the statewide coordinating and support structure for distance education, and the state has addressed two of the key issues that often face educational consortiums: a common course numbering system and a standard tuition rate across all institutions. Wyoming is the ninth largest state in terms of square miles and it is the least populated. This setting emphasizes the importance of access to both educational programs and educational services via distance technologies. Recognizing this need, WyDEC hosts an annual conference focusing on best practices in distance instruction and providing student services at a distance.

NEW DIRECTIONS FOR COMMUNITY COLLEGES • DOI: 10.1002/cc

Employing a mutually beneficial focus, WyDEC has been able to coordinate distance education programs, student services, and instructional support with attention placed on quality, cost-effectiveness, and innovation. The consortium has also been able to help the participating community colleges meet faculty capacity concerns in terms of the shared costs of curricular development and faculty development, enabling the institutions to move from offering courses to offering degree programs.

Rural community colleges must also consider student access to the Internet and the availability of broadband connection. As already noted, Internet penetration in rural areas continues to lag slightly behind suburban and urban locales, and even more importantly, less than one-fourth of rural residents have broadband connection to the Internet. Therefore, very few community colleges use high-bandwidth technologies in courses delivered via the Internet. Johnson and others (2004) sought to identify how the Internet was used in course delivery. Responses to their survey indicated that the most frequent technology application used in Internet-based distance education was e-mail (94.3 percent), followed by course management systems (84.2 percent), and asynchronous discussion lists (64.2 percent). The least used applications were broadband-based, such as voice chat (13.7 percent), desktop videoconferencing (16.1 percent), streaming video (37.7 percent), streaming audio (44.5 percent), and streaming PowerPoint (47.3 percent).

Based on these findings, Johnson and others (2004) suggest that colleges may be purposely selecting low-bandwidth technologies so that individuals who do not have broadband access can still participate in distance education programs. Moreover, instructional technology specialists have concluded that course design and pedagogy are more important factors than the specific technology used in distance education programming (Phipps and Merisotis, 1999). As Internet access penetrates further into rural areas, and dial-up connections are able to receive low-bandwidth applications, there appears to be continued opportunity for growth in distance enrollments at rural locations. Therefore, rural community colleges should focus on using low-bandwidth technologies to provide access to distance education to the greatest number of individuals and realize that broadband technologies do not, in themselves, provide for a *better* distance education course.

In order to gain the significant commitment from policymakers and funding agencies necessary to develop a technological infrastructure and incorporate distance education technologies, rural community colleges may need to assume an even greater role in economic and community development. The Rural Community College Initiative (MDC, Inc., 2001) is crafted from a catalyst-based philosophy where community colleges foster and facilitate collaborations and coalitions between themselves and other organizations in their community or region. The organizations work together to build better communities by developing sustainable economies through lifelong educational access and opportunity. As a single entity, the rural community college may not have the financial resources necessary to purchase the infrastructure and technology required to comprehensively embrace and benefit from distance programming. However, serving as an intermediary, community colleges can build cost-effective coalitions with schools, businesses and industry, and economic development entities to garner sufficient support from policymakers and sufficient funding to create community and regional infrastructures that provide rural residents with greater access to the Internet and broadband connections.

Next Steps

There do not appear to be many short-term steps that will significantly affect distance learning in rural community colleges. An initial step might involve strategies to improve access to computers and broadband Internet connection. A number of concerns have been raised about passing the costs of technology to students, either by requiring the purchase of a computer or adding a student technology fee. Katsinas and Moeck (2002) point to leasing, rather than purchasing, as one strategy to provide additional computers for student use. Establishing broadband connections in public campus areas with extended hours, such as the library and student union, would promote the use of laptop computers. Allowing community members who do not have broadband connections at home or work to bring laptops to these campus locations would help develop coalitions and document needs for the long term. A second short-term step is to improve the technological capacity of faculty and students. Economies of scale might be realized by partnering with K–12 schools, libraries, health care facilities, and business and industry on common training needs and perhaps sharing personnel costs. In addition, developing programs to provide end-user support will be necessary as rural institutions look to expand distance offerings.

None of these suggestions, however, addresses the problem of expanding rural students' ability to benefit from distance education. Two distinct, long-term recommendations are necessary to accomplish such a goal. The first involves curricular development. It is important that rural community colleges develop a broader selection of distance course offerings, including technical and vocational courses, and that students are able to complete certificates and degrees through distance technologies. Existing consortia should emphasize a macro approach leading to the development of distance certificates and degrees rather than continuing a micro approach of simply adding more courses. Commercial vendors should be encouraged to focus on curricular gaps, especially when members of the consortium do not have the disciplinary expertise or the capacity to develop an Internet-based curriculum.

The second recommendation is for rural community colleges to develop a long-term strategy and the necessary support to convince policymakers to address the digital divide between rural and urban and suburban communities. Chesson and Rubin (2002) stress that educational policy is primarily a state responsibility, and community colleges are primarily local entities. Katsinas and Moeck (2002) point out, however, that the doctrine of universal service resulted from federal policy. In developing a state policy framework for rural community colleges, Chesson and Rubin stress three points regarding technology: an adequate infrastructure to support distance education and high-speed Internet access; responsibility to a public or quasi-public agency to extend affordable Internet access to rural communities; and baseline funding to provide ongoing financial resources for rural community colleges to maintain technological capacity.

The Internet has become the most common delivery source for distance education, and soon the majority of urban and suburban residents will access the Internet through broadband connections. Most Internet-based distance education offerings do not currently use broadband applications, but the boom in the number of courses using podcasts is only one indication that current practice is likely to change. Moreover, the move to a global economy emphasizes the need for state-of-the-art technological competence among all community college students. For these reasons, dialogue about extending Internet access to rural communities and their residents must focus on access by broadband connection. Back in 1995 Bill Gates suggested including access to the Internet in the doctrine of universal service—but this strategy or other cost-effective strategies to extend broadband in remote areas have not been put in place.

Funding to develop an infrastructure and maintain technological capacity is also a policy concern. Rural community colleges simply do not have the necessary fiscal and human resources to serve as the sole computer and Internet providers in their communities, provide adequate training for the various constituencies, and initiate and maintain comprehensive distance education programming. Chesson and Rubin (2002) emphasize that funding for community colleges varies between states and between the community college districts within states. Often rural community colleges are at a financial disadvantage, and lack the fiscal resources necessary to design and implement an infrastructure as well as establish a sufficient operating budget for the continued expenditures necessary for maintaining and replacing hardware and software.

One way to inform policymakers and increase support inside and across state lines is to illustrate the numerous efforts of rural community colleges to develop telecommunications infrastructure, facilitate Internet access, and promote technology applications for their region. Case studies of projects funded in the Rural Community College Initiative (www.mdcinc.org/rcci/), the ongoing work of the Rural Community College Alliance (http://www.ruralcommunitycolleges.org), and resources available through the Rural Policy Roundtable of the American Association of Community Colleges (http://www.aacc.nche.edu) are valuable to any efforts to influence policy.

Butzen and Liston (2003) stress that rural community colleges need to become advocacy leaders in developing long-term solutions to the digital divide. They provide three recommendations on how these institutions can advocate for better Internet and technology resources: they can promote the potential benefits of advanced technologies in community forums and to community and business leaders; they can assess community needs for access and training; and they can establish partnerships with local offices of federal agencies, business and industry, schools, hospitals, and libraries to aggregate the demand of both public and private entities. The authors also recommend that community colleges take a leadership role in developing community-wide strategic plans regarding technology.

A sustained effort will be necessary for policy development to become policy action. The Internet has become an essential part of our society and is the dominant technology in providing distance education. Rural communities have yet to benefit from affordable high-speed Internet access, and rural community colleges do not have the necessary resources to bridge this gap. Until state and federal policy addresses the disparity between urban and suburban and rural areas, most rural community colleges and their constituencies will not realize the full potential of distance education.

References

Allen, I. E., and Seaman, J. *Sizing the Opportunity: The Quality and Extent of Online Education in the United States, 2002 and 2003.* Needham, Mass.: Sloan Consortium, 2003.

Allen, I. E., and Seaman, J. *Entering the Mainstream: The Quality and Extent of Online Education in the United States, 2003 and 2004.* Needham, Mass.: Sloan Consortium, 2004.

Allen, I. E., and Seaman, J. *Growing by Degrees: Online Education in the United States, 2005.* Needham, Mass.: Sloan Consortium, 2005.

Bell, P., Reddy, P., and Rainie, L. *Rural Areas and the Internet.* Washington, D.C.: Pew Internet and American Life Project, 2004. http://www.pewinternet.org/report_display.asp?r=112. Accessed Nov. 30, 2006.

Block, M. *Widening the Internet Highway to Rural America.* Washington, D.C.: National Public Radio, Dec. 2005. http://www.npr.org/templates/story/story.php?storyId=5053488. Accessed Nov. 30, 2006.

Burnell, G. "Courses You Teach, Resources They Need." *Community College Week,* 2002, *14*(15), 14.

Butzen, S., and Liston, C. D. "Rural Community Colleges and the Digital Divide." *Learning Abstracts,* 2003, *6*(5). http://www.league.org/publication/abstracts/learning/lelabs0305.htm. Accessed Nov. 30, 2006.

Cejda, B. D. "Distance Education in Rural Community Colleges." *Community College Journal of Research and Practice,* forthcoming.

Chesson, J. P., Jr., and Rubin, S. *Toward Rural Prosperity: A State Policy Framework in Support of Rural Community Colleges.* Chapel Hill, N.C.: MDC, Inc., 2002. http://www.mdcinc.org/rcci/towardruralprosperity.pdf. Assessed Nov. 30, 2006.

Epper, R. M., and Garn, M. *Virtual College & University Consortia: A National Study.* Boulder, Colo.: State Higher Education Executive Officers, 2003. http://www.sheeo.org/disted/vcu.pdf. Accessed Nov. 30, 2006.

Free Press. *Community Internet: Broadband as a Public Service.* Northampton, Mass.: Free Press, 2005. http://www.freepress.net/communityinternet/. Accessed Nov. 30, 2006.

Gallagher, S. *Distance Learning at the Tipping Point: Critical Success Factors to Growing Fully Online Distance Learning Programs.* Boston: Eduventures, Inc., 2002.

Gates, B. *The Road Ahead.* New York: Viking, 1995.

Glass, V., Talluto, S., and Babb, C. "Technological Breakthroughs Lower the Cost of Broadband Service to Isolated Customers." *Government Information Quarterly,* 2003, *20,* 121–133.

Horrigan, J., and Murray, K. *Rural Broadband Internet Use.* Washington, D.C.: Pew Internet & American Life Project, 2006. http://www.pewinternet.org/pdfs/PIP_Rural_Broadband.pdf. Assessed Nov. 30, 2006.

Johnson, S. D., and others. "Internet-Based Learning in Postsecondary Career and Technical Education." *Journal of Vocational Education Research,* 2004, *29*(2), 101–121.

Katsinas, S. G., and Moeck, P. "The Digital Divide and Rural Community Colleges: Problems and Prospects." *Community College Journal of Research and Practice,* 2002, *26*(3), 207–224.

Kinley, E. R. "Implementing Distance Education, the Impact of Institutional Characteristics: A View from the Department Chair's Chair." Unpublished doctoral dissertation, University of Nebraska-Lincoln, 2001.

MacBrayne, P. S. "Distance Education: The Way of the Future for Rural Community Colleges." In J. Killacky and J. R. Valadez (eds.), *Portrait of the Rural Community College.* New Directions for Community Colleges, no. 90. San Francisco: Jossey-Bass, 1995.

MDC, Inc. *Expanding Economic and Educational Opportunity in Distressed Rural Areas: A Conceptual Framework for the Rural Community College Initiative.* Chapel Hill, N.C.: MDC, Inc., 2001.

O'Quinn, L., and Corry, M. "Factors That Deter Faculty from Participating in Distance Education." *Online Journal of Distance Learning Administration,* 2002, *5*(4), 1–18.

Phipps, R., and Merisotis, J. *What's the Difference? A Review of Contemporary Research on the Effectiveness of Distance Learning in Higher Education.* Washington, D.C.: Institute for Higher Education Policy, 1999. http://www.ihep.com/Pubs/PDF/Difference.pdf. Assessed Nov. 30, 2006.

Roberson, T. J., and Klotz, J. "How Can Instructors and Administrators Fill the Missing Link in Online Instruction?" *Online Journal of Distance Learning Administration,* 2002, *5*(4), 1–7.

Sink, D. W., and Jackson, K. L. "Bridging the Digital Divide: A Collaborative Approach." *Community College Journal,* 2000, *71*(2), 38–41.

U.S. Department of Education. *The Condition of Education 2002.* NCES 2002–025. Washington, D.C.: U.S. Department of Education, National Center for Education Statistics, 2002.

Waits, T., and Lewis, L. *Distance Education at Degree-Granting Postsecondary Institutions: 2000–2001.* NCES 2003–017. Washington, D.C.: U.S. Department of Education, National Center for Education Statistics, 2003.

Wu, Y., and Turner, P. "The Relationship of Bandwidth, Interaction, and Performance in Online Classes: A Study." *Online Journal of Distance Learning Administration,* 2006, *9*(1).

Wyoming Community College Distance Education Task Force. *Wyoming Community Colleges: Responding to the Growing Need for Distance Education.* Cheyenne: Wyoming Community College Commission, 2004. (ED 483 288)

BRENT D. CEJDA *is associate professor in the Department of Educational Administration at the University of Nebraska-Lincoln and executive director of the National Council of Instructional Administrators.*

This chapter reviews the strategies described in this volume that rural college leaders can use to address the issues and challenges their institutions face.

Strategizing for the Future

Pamela L. Eddy, John P. Murray

This volume provides a context to better understand the issues rural community colleges face. In creating strategies for the future, institutional leaders should think about leadership differently and establish institutional collaborations to share resources and address community issues. Given the graying of the professoriate (Berry, Hammons, and Denny, 2001) and predicted leadership turnovers (Shults, 2001), it is also important to consider how rural community colleges will compete in attracting faculty and leaders to a rural locale. Finally, it is important to consider how policymakers can help rural colleges effectively enhance economic development.

Meeting Personnel Needs

Strategies for meeting these challenges include the up-front acknowledgment of what it means to work in a rural location. Clearly written job announcements that articulate the cultural context of the college's location and the challenges of working in these areas are essential. Articulating a more accurate picture of what it means to work in a remote region of the country will lessen the surprise some outsiders may have upon finding themselves working and living in a small town.

Rural colleges must also have a clear understanding of their institutional goals, mission, and vision. The time spent in institutional self-reflection will enable search committees to be clear about what they are seeking in faculty and staff candidates and what qualities a successful

candidate should bring to the position. A part of this process is the creation of job descriptions that accurately portray the demands of the position.

Rural colleges can think of creative ways to share faculty and leaders, especially if they are located within a reasonable drive of a more urban location. More online course delivery options allow faculty members to increase their support system by collaborating with other faculty at other institutions. Faculty development efforts may also be supported by working with regional universities and partnering on programming. Likewise, leadership development can be structured in collaboration with others in the state or region. The leadership development partnership coordinated by the Mid-South Partnership for Rural Community Colleges (see Chapter Five) provides a framework for collaborative efforts to establish a "grow-your-own" leadership development process. The exposure to other practices in such a system would begin to develop potential leaders with a larger worldview and a wider network of colleagues and mentors to tap into.

Institutional Collaborations

Collaborations and partnerships are helpful in supporting rural faculty and leaders. Partnering allows for resource sharing and building institutional capacity. Partnerships may cut across institutional lines and reach out to K–12 districts in the region. Even though the context of teaching and leading differs among institutional types, shared development on fundamental issues of learning pedagogy, leadership strategies, and institutional planning can bring a different perspective. These types of collaborations can build bridges between institutions and troubleshoot issues that continue to plague community college education, including student underpreparedness and remediation.

The small resource base and total demand for products in rural institutions often disallows economies of scale, especially when it comes to technology. Partnering with other colleges or school districts can increase purchasing power. This more systemic approach to resource challenges allows for savings and offers the potential to restructure the current, separate efforts of educational institutions located in the same region. The increased demand for seamless educational programming provides an incentive for looking at how educational systems can work together to increase student learning and ultimately meet community needs.

As noted elsewhere in this volume, faculty development at community colleges relies on the work of a few campus members. Partnering can increase programming options and aid in cost sharing. Technology can put faculty development modules online for easier access—resulting in an increased pool of participants. An example of this is the Texas Collaborative for Teaching Excellence (http://www.texascollaborative.org), a statewide professional development network for community and technical college faculty. Programs offered include an academy for part-time faculty, development workshops on teaching and learning topics, and online resources for faculty.

As already noted, leadership development can be accomplished through a "grow-your-own" program, as described in Chapter Five. The regional approach taken by the MidSouth Partnership for Rural Community Colleges links community colleges with academic programs to prepare future leaders. Identifying future leaders in the rural community college itself is the first step in this process. Given the need to match leader candidates to the environment, the grow-your-own-leaders strategy makes sense, because these potential leaders already understand what it means to work in a rural environment. Critical to this strategy, however, is the identification of potential leaders. Often individuals do not aspire for higher-level positions, and instead seek these positions as a result of being tapped or mentored (Mitchell, 2005). It is important to consider who might be overlooked because of gender, race, or institutional location. A process should be in place that is open for self-selection but also looks at the ways in which individuals can be identified for inclusion. Without this inclusion process, a number of potential leaders may be lost.

University preparation programs play an integral role in preparing future community college leaders. During the growth years of the community college, a larger number of programs were available to foster community college leadership development. Resurgence in these types of programs is taking place (Bragg, 2002). As universities work with community colleges to develop programming to meet future leadership shortfalls, it is important to consider the course content. These programs must cover the needs of rural communities: fewer resources, social ills associated with poverty, and so forth. Background on the sociology of rural development and working with rural residents is important to better understand the rural college context.

The community college's role in economic development and community outreach is of heightened importance in rural areas, because these colleges are often major employers in their regions, the convening location for cultural events, key partners in collaborations, and viewed as a link to a better future by students and businesses alike. Greater community expectations of rural colleges in reform and change efforts create opportunities but also pressures that can lead to greater risk of failure. College and community leaders need to develop a vision and strategic plan for these institutions that is based on a realistic perspective of what they can accomplish. Key to this type of planning is, ultimately, making hard decisions about what the rural college can and cannot do for its constituents. A plan focused on a few key changes or goals may better serve local communities than a more ambitious one. Community partners may pick up some of the programming that the rural college no longer can perform—for instance, lifelong learning classes may be offered by the public school community outreach office or county extension offices. A regional planning effort would help the college develop a comprehensive plan on educational needs, thereby allowing a determination of what programs it may best offer. A regional plan would allow the college to focus on programming, knowing that regional partners would pick up areas that it is not covering. More change can occur at the involved

regional campuses since the leverage for change is greater with more partners providing programming. Individual campuses can then pick and chose
what is of most benefit to their campus members.

Again, most critical is that college leaders think in a systemic manner
and frame the required changes in a variety of ways so that they can gain
support from diverse constituents (Eddy, 2003).

Policy Considerations

Policymakers at the state and federal levels need to address the "rural differential" and the inequities caused for rural dwellers. Making allowances
for the differential begins to provide rural communities with an opportunity
to help themselves. Because rural community colleges are central meeting
places for their communities, they provide a key conduit for state funding
to be funneled to remote areas and to address local problems.

To keep graduates in the rural community, business and industry must
provide employment opportunities. The smaller locations often mean that
entrepreneurs or small businesses are more successful than they might be elsewhere (Brown, 2003; Appalachian Regional Commission, 2000). Thus, developing incubators for fledgling businesses can help spark an economic
renaissance in these areas. Rural colleges could benefit from policies allowing
tax breaks for such new operations. Rural colleges may find that collaborating
with other institutions in the region may lead to greater funding opportunities
and increase their ability to obtain grants. Loan deferments for individuals who
take positions in rural areas can help bring in needed skill bases. In the past,
educators, business leaders, and physicians have received loan deferments or
fulfillments if they made a commitment to work in a particular region or with
a specific population; this strategy can also be employed in rural areas.

Thus, programs to aid rural colleges are needed in several key areas.
First, economic development requires a regional approach. Community partners, governmental agencies, health providers, and public educators need to
pool resources to address common problems. Second, policymakers and institutional leaders should develop a needs assessment that identifies key educational areas required to support the economic development and public
demand for services. Finally, state, federal, and corporate giving can begin to
provide funding for critical programs that address the planning process and
implementation of the coordinated efforts already outlined. Rural community
colleges can be the key champions that pull together these combined efforts
because they act as prime community centers and leaders in their regions.

The issues faced by rural community colleges are persistent and provide unique challenges. However, not all rural institutions face the same
issues or in the same way. As noted in Chapter One, large rural community
colleges show striking similarities to those located in suburban areas. A reason for this might be that the rural areas that support larger institutions are
in fact expansions of the metropolitan areas, signifying another ring in the

circle emanating from urban centers. Thus, midsized and smaller rural colleges are in more dire straits than their larger rural counterparts because they have fewer economic resources generated from tuition and their communities are located further from urban employment centers. It is important to provide policies to support those with the greatest need. Meanwhile, the closer proximity of larger rural institutions and suburban community colleges argues for intentional bridge building between these two institutional types.

Lessons for Urban and Suburban Community Colleges

Urban and suburban colleges could look to their rural counterparts to determine areas of increased efficiencies. As noted throughout this volume, employees at rural locations often hold multiple positions and responsibilities. Best practices in rural schools might spur improvements in urban areas. "Grow-your-own" programs for faculty and leadership development can be replicated on urban and suburban campuses, for example. Urban colleges can borrow tactics from leadership development programs such as these, which are described in this volume. Working with area colleges can help provide support for current employees and also help in the recruitment of needed expertise in urban community colleges. However, prospective leaders and faculty alike need to understand their work context. Like rural community colleges, urban colleges should be clear with prospective employees about what it is like to work in their locales. Just as some individuals may be surprised at what it means to work in a rural environment, some may be surprised when they find themselves in an urban location. Not all the lessons outlined in this volume will translate to urban areas, but many will. Increased sharing across institutional types can aid both rural and urban community colleges on an institutional level and from an individual perspective.

Future Directions for Rural Community College Practice, Policy, and Research

Ultimately, it is important to recognize the problems faced by rural colleges and work to alleviate those we can. This volume has attempted to provide some insights to help readers on this journey. Several critical issues are on the horizon for rural community colleges. First, pending retirements will severely affect these community colleges because they represent 60 percent of all community colleges. Replacing these retiring leaders will be an immediate challenge. As Leist explains in Chapter Four, it is critical to create truthful advertisements for new rural presidents. Candidates need to understand the issues they will face when taking the helm at a rural institution, and in particular, the issues they will face on the individual campus. Again, one way to replace vacant leadership positions is to develop a grow-your-own program in conjunction with regional universities. Recruiting faculty is another pressing need for rural community colleges. Like the search for new presidents, faculty searches should outline what it means to work with students on a rural campus and what it means to work in a rural locale. Once new faculty are hired, it is critical to provide them with support through faculty development programs.

Rural areas have been hard hit by economic downturns. Agriculture, mining, and small industries have all faced losses that ultimately affect these regions. Policies that address the rural differential in governmental funding and support can provide a needed jump-start for some rural areas. It is also necessary to establish partnerships and make collaborative efforts to address the critical issues in rural areas, but these partnerships will need to take a regional approach with a systems perspective. This orientation will allow for more holistic solutions.

The creation of the new Carnegie classification system (Carnegie Foundation for the Advancement of Teaching, 2005) allows for research focused on rural community colleges. The ability to disaggregate data based on institutional location and size provides a means to look more closely at concerns about students, faculty, and leaders. Areas for future research include best practices for the formation of regional collaborations to address common rural problems, the leadership approaches of rural presidents, alternative opportunities for faculty development, implication of technology in rural areas, best practices for community outreach, retention and transfer issues for rural community college students, and means to support economic development in the region. Together, the findings from this research will aid those leading, guiding, and supporting rural community colleges.

Sources and Information

The following are some significant writings on issues faced by rural community colleges. These works, which provide a portrait of the rural community college context and how individuals in these locales are navigating the challenges, offer information of relevance to college leaders, faculty, students, and support staff. Several Internet sites listed provide access to specific information on rural issues.

Internet Sources

American Association of Community Colleges. *Rural Public Policy Roundtable*. Washington, D.C.: American Association of Community Colleges. http://www.aacc.nche.edu/Content/NavigationMenu/AboutAACC/Rural_P olicy_Roundtable/Rural_Policy_Roundtable.htm. Assessed Nov. 30, 2006.

Rural Community College Alliance. Meridian, Miss.: MidSouth Partnership for Rural Community Colleges. http://www.ruralcommunitycolleges.org/. Accessed Nov. 30, 2006.

Rural Community College Initiative. Meridian, Miss.: Mississippi State University. http://srdc.msstate.edu/rcci/. Accessed Nov. 30, 2006.
Rural Policy Institute. Columbia: University of Missouri. http://www.rupri.org/. Accessed Nov. 30, 2006.

Faculty

Murray, J. P. "Meeting the Needs of New Faculty at Rural Community Colleges." *Community College Journal of Research and Practice,* 2005, *29,* 215–232.
Wolfe, J. R., and Strange, C. C. "Academic Life at the Franchise: Faculty Culture in a Rural Two-Year Branch Campus." *Review of Higher Education,* 2003, *26*(3), 343–362.

College Leaders

Amey, M. J., and Laden, B. (eds.). *Conceptualizing Leadership as Learning* [Special issue]. *Community College Journal of Research and Practice,* 2005, *29*(9–10).
Lovell, N., Crittenden, L., Davis, M., and Stumpf, D. "The Road Less Traveled: Atypical Doctoral Preparation of Leaders in Rural Community Colleges." *Community College Journal of Research and Practice,* 2003, *27*(1), 1–14.

Students

Anderson, P. J. "A Study of the Transfer Process at a Small, Rural Community College." Unpublished doctoral dissertation, University of North Carolina-Greensboro, 2005.
Killacky, J., and Valadez, J. R. (eds.). *Portrait of the Rural Community College.* New Directions for Community Colleges, no. 90. San Francisco: Jossey-Bass, 1995.
Poole, J. S. "Predictors of Persistent Black Male Students' Commitment to Rural Mississippi Two-Year Public Institutions." Unpublished doctoral dissertation, Mississippi State University, 2006.

Institutional Issues and Outreach

Butzen, S., and Liston, C. D. "Rural Community Colleges and the Digital Divide." *Learning Abstracts,* 2003, *6*(5). http://www.league.org/publication/abstracts/learning/lelabs0305.htm. Assessed Nov. 30, 2006.
Eller, R., Martinez, R., Pace, C., Pavel, M., and Barnett, L. *Rural Community College Initiative IV: Capacity for Leading Institutional and Community Change.* Report No. AACC-PB-99-3. Washington, D.C.: American Association of Community Colleges, 1999. (ED 432 332)
Katsinas, S. G., Alexander, K. F., and Opp, R. D. *Preserving Access with Excellence: Financing for Rural Community Colleges.* Rural Community College Initiative Policy Paper. Chapel Hill, N.C.: MDC, Inc., 2003.
McJunkin, K. S. "Rural Community Colleges: An Overview of the Issues. UCLA Community College Bibliography." *Community College Journal of Research and Practice,* 2005, *29*(5), 411–417.

Miller, M. T., and Tuttle, C. C. *How Rural Community Colleges Develop Their Communities and the People Who Live in Them. Report of the MidSouth Partnership for Rural Community Colleges.* Starkville, Miss.: MidSouth Partnership for Rural Community Colleges and the Stennis Institute for Government, 2006.

References

Appalachian Regional Commission. "Tools for Entrepreneurship: Building New Economies in Rural America." Conference Proceedings, Clermont County, Ohio, Sept. 17–19, 2000. (ED 467 310)

Berry, L. H., Hammons, J. O., and Denny, G. S. "Faculty Retirement Turnover in Community Colleges: A Real or Imagined Problem?" *Community College Journal of Research and Practice,* 2001, *25,* 123–136.

Bragg, D. D. "Doing Their Best: Exemplary Graduate Leadership Programs." *Community College Journal,* Aug.-Sept. 2002, pp. 49–53.

Brown, B. L. *The Role of CTE in Entrepreneurship. ERIC Digest.* Columbus: The Ohio State University, Eric Clearinghouse on Adult, Career, and Vocational Education, 2003. (ED 482 537)

Carnegie Foundation for the Advancement of Teaching. *The Carnegie Classification of Institutions of Higher Education.* Stanford, Calif.: Carnegie Foundation for the Advancement of Teaching, 2005. http://www.carnegiefoundation.org/classifications/. Accessed Nov. 30, 2006.

Eddy, P. L. "Sensemaking on Campus: How Community College Presidents Frame Change." *Community College Journal of Research and Practice,* 2003, 27(6), 453–471.

Mitchell, R. "Work-Life Balance." Paper presented at the 2005 annual conference of the Association for the Study of Higher Education in Philadelphia, 2005.

Shults, C. *The Critical Impact of Impending Retirements on Community College Leadership.* Leadership Series Research Brief No. 1. Washington, D.C.: American Association of Community Colleges, 2001.

PAMELA L. EDDY *is associate professor of higher education and doctoral program coordinator in education leadership at Central Michigan University.*

JOHN P. MURRAY *is professor of higher education at Texas Tech University and program director for the higher education administration program.*

INDEX

competition for scarce resources. Chapter authors give guidelines for fundraising, corporate partnerships, grants for workforce development, mill levy elections, realigning budget priorities, and the key skills that today's community college presidents need.

ISBN: 0-7879-8364-0

CC131 **Community College Student Affairs: What Really Matters**
Steven R. Helfgot, Marguerite M. Culp
Uses the results of a national survey to identify the major challenges and opportunities for student affairs practitioners in community colleges, and describes the most effective strategies for meeting challenges. Chapters discuss core values, cultures of evidence, faculty partnerships, career counseling, and support for underrepresented populations, plus assessment tools and best practices in student affairs.

ISBN: 0-7879-8332-2

CC130 **Critical Thinking: Unfinished Business**
Christine M. McMahon
With a few exceptions, critical thinking is not being effectively taught nor even correctly understood in higher education. This volume advocates for professional development in critical thinking to engage all members of the campus community. It presents blueprints for such development, plus practical case studies from campuses already doing it. Also covers classroom assignments, solutions to resistance, and program assessment.

ISBN: 0-7879-8185-0

CC129 **Responding to the Challenges of Developmental Education**
Carol A. Kozeracki
Approximately 40 percent of incoming community college students enroll in developmental math, English, or reading courses. Despite the availability of popular models for teaching these classes, community colleges continue to struggle with effectively educating underprepared students, who have a wide variety of backgrounds. This volume discusses the dangers of isolating developmental education from the broader college; provides examples of successful programs; offers recommendations adaptable to different campuses; and identifies areas for future research.

ISBN: 0-7879-8050-1

CC128 **From Distance Education to E-Learning: Lessons Along the Way**
Beverly L. Bower, Kimberly P. Hardy
Correspondence, telecourses, and now e-learning: distance education continues to grow and change. This volume's authors examine what community colleges must do to make distance education successful, including meeting technology challenges, containing costs, developing campuswide systems, teaching effectively, balancing faculty workloads, managing student services, and redesigning courses for online learning. Includes case studies from colleges, plus state and regional policy perspectives.

ISBN: 0-7879-7927-9

NEW DIRECTIONS FOR COMMUNITY COLLEGES
Order Form
SUBSCRIPTIONS AND SINGLE ISSUES

DISCOUNTED BACK ISSUES:

Use this form to receive **20% off** all back issues of New Directions for Community Colleges. All single issues priced at **$23.20** (normally $29.00)

TITLE	ISSUE NO.	ISBN

Call 888-378-2537 or see mailing instructions below. When calling, mention the promotional code, JB7ND, to receive your discount.

SUBSCRIPTIONS: *(1 year, 4 issues)*

□ New Order   □ Renewal

U.S.	□ Individual: $80	□ Institutional: $195
Canada/Mexico	□ Individual: $80	□ Institutional: $235
All Others	□ Individual: $104	□ Institutional: $269

Call 888-378-2537 or see mailing and pricing instructions below. Online subscriptions are available at www.interscience.wiley.com.

Copy or detach page and send to:
John Wiley & Sons, Journals Dept, 5th Floor
989 Market Street, San Francisco, CA 94103-1741

Order Form can also be faxed to: 888-481-2665

Issue/Subscription Amount: $ _____
Shipping Amount: $ _____
(for single issues only—subscription prices include shipping)
Total Amount: $ _____

SHIPPING CHARGES:		
SURFACE	Dometic	Canadian
First Item	$5.00	$6.00
Each Add'l Item	$3.00	$1.50

(No sales tax for U.S. subscriptions. Canadian residents, add GST for subscription orders. Individual rate subscriptions must be paid by personal check or credit card. Individual rate subscriptions may not be resold as library copies.)

□ Payment enclosed (U.S. check or money order only. All payments must be in U.S. dollars.)

□ VISA   □ MC   □ Amex # _____ Exp. Date_____

Card Holder Name _____ Card Issue # _____

Signature_____ Day Phone _____

□ Bill Me (U.S. institutional orders only. Purchase order required.)

Purchase order # _____
Federal Tax ID13559302   GST 89102 8052

Name_____

Address _____

Phone _____ E-mail _____

JB7ND

NEW DIRECTIONS FOR COMMUNITY COLLEGES IS NOW AVAILABLE ONLINE AT WILEY INTERSCIENCE

What is Wiley InterScience?

Wiley InterScience is the dynamic online content service from John Wiley & Sons delivering the full text of over 300 leading scientific, technical, medical, and professional journals, plus major reference works, the acclaimed *Current Protocols* laboratory manuals, and even the full text of select Wiley print books online.

What are some special features of Wiley InterScience?

Wiley InterScience Alerts is a service that delivers table of contents via e-mail for any journal available on Wiley InterScience as soon as a new issue is published online.
Early View is Wiley's exclusive service presenting individual articles online as soon as they are ready, even before the release of the compiled print issue. These articles are complete, peer-reviewed, and citable.
CrossRef is the innovative multi-publisher reference linking system enabling readers to move seamlessly from a reference in a journal article to the cited publication, typically located on a different server and published by a different publisher.

How can I access Wiley InterScience?

Visit http://www.interscience.wiley.com

Guest Users can browse Wiley InterScience for unrestricted access to journal Tables of Contents and Article Abstracts, or use the powerful search engine.
Registered Users are provided with a *Personal Home Page* to store and manage customized alerts, searches, and links to favorite journals and articles. Additionally, Registered Users can view free Online Sample Issues and preview selected material from major reference works.
Licensed Customers are entitled to access full-text journal articles in PDF, with select journals also offering full-text HTML.

How do I become an Authorized User?

Authorized Users are individuals authorized by a paying Customer to have access to the journals in Wiley InterScience. For example, a university that subscribes to Wiley journals is considered to be the Customer. Faculty, staff and students authorized by the university to have access to those journals in Wiley InterScience are Authorized Users. Users should contact their Library for information on which Wiley journals they have access to in Wiley InterScience.

ASK YOUR INSTITUTION ABOUT WILEY INTERSCIENCE TODAY!